Rose Hunt
the blind Navajo
Nov 8. 2008

*A true story about faith, hope, prayer, and love*

# Finding Helen ~ A Navajo Miracle

**By: Rose W. Johnson-Tsosie**

Published by:
Bluewater Publications
1812 CR 111
Killen, Alabama 35645
www.BluewaterPublications.com

*Dedicated to...*

*F. Albert & Wilmont Johnson Family in
Heaven and on Earth.*

*The Frank Tsosie Family and all his clan.*

*The Helen Morgan Tsosie/Ben Family and all her clan.*

*Special thanks to Mary Annette Stanners, my twin sister, whom I love so very
much and with whom I cherish many childhood memories.*

*My great appreciation to Gordon V. Johnson, my brother, who kept his
family strong in faith, hope, dreams of eternal happiness, and loved his twin
sisters.*

*To my many friends and mentors throughout my life, thank you.*

# CONTENTS

# PROLOGUE

My physical body was frozen motionless as I stared at myself in the rearview mirror. I thought, "Well I'm here, and I'm okay with that; now if I can take one more bold step forward." True, it's taken 33 years to stand at the pinnacle of life… my life. I told myself, "Rose, just breathe!" In reality I couldn't turn back now, not even if I wanted to, as it seemed the heavenly forces had lifted me up and placed me here without me even trying. Besides I've traveled such a distance to be here.

A moment later, I found myself standing directly in front of the old wooden door of a Navajo Hogan. I knocked hard, fearful I would not be heard; then I waited impatiently. My heart was pounding loudly as if it were a drum. I consciously held my breath for a second or two, as if that helped any. My hands were notably shaking with excitement. Within my heart I pleaded silently to God. "Please, let someone open the door!"

I stood as a stranger; my mind was actively involved in trying to see beyond the plaid curtain that obscured my view of what awaited me on the other side of the door. I could tell the humble existence was present. I questioned the road of indifference and yet found myself oddly familiar being here for the first time. Could it be I was always meant to be here?

# SECTION I

## *Chapter 1: Helen's 13<sup>th</sup> Birthday*

Helen celebrated her 13th birthday on one of the worst winter days in a long time. Her mother Mabel made a blue-cornbread cake and put one candle on the top. Her sister, Mary, along with Mabel and Helen excitedly shared a small piece of cake with her extended family, then started to play a game of cards which all enjoyed no matter what the occasion.

The cold brisk air sneaking through the cracks of the door made her want to stay in the Hogan by the pot belly stove. While the family festivities continued around her, Helen's mind began to drift. She felt so awkward being already married and pregnant at her age, yet unaware of the complexities of life. Her maternal feelings became more apparent as she was in her eighth month of pregnancy.

Her mother Mabel hadn't told her much about pregnancy. What should she be experiencing? How would she learn about giving birth? It seemed to Helen that she was just too young to think of bringing life into the world. Helen knew the Navajo traditional ways. At the tender age of 13, she was considered a woman. What was expected of her as a young Navajo bride did little to calm her fears.

Helen was no stranger to difficult conditions. All her brothers and sisters lived in one small "female" Hogan which was dedicated for the family by the medicine man. The home itself was pre-hexagon shaped, with wood sticks holding up the structure and clay mud covering the sticks. A cast-iron wood burning stove was in the center of the home. Several of the family's Navajo rugs were spread out on the earth floors to help keep the place clean and warmer when the cold weather came knocking at their door. The little hogan had no electricity or running water; it was like living in a third-world country within the United States.

Helen loved watching the sunrise from the door of the Hogan. Once outside, two narrow paths marked the way. One led to the small wooden outhouse. When the wind blew, you could hear the door screech as it hung loosely on one hinge. The other path led to the sheep pen and horse corral. Sheep were an important part of the family livelihood as they provided food for the family and their wool was used to make blankets and rugs to sell. The horses were a prized possession among her people. Several of her brothers won money and trophies when rodeo time came at various locations throughout the Navajo nation.

Helen's family would have to travel by horse and wagon down to the Whitewater Springs to collect water from a well and then haul the water back to the Hogan to use for both family and animals. The water was contained in a 50-gallon wooden barrel, which would last for one week. It was hard work to siphon water from the frozen spring. As they worked together hauling water, the hard work became easier to endure and strengthened bonds among the family.

After collecting the water, the ride home was long and Helen often sat on the tailgate dangling her legs over the edge of the wagon gate. Sometimes she would just let her feet drag on the dirt roads. This time, due to her condition, she sat against the buckboard of the wagon watching the snow fall on the muddy road as they left behind the four wheel tracks.

Often while driving the wagon her husband glanced back and smiled. Frank was a quiet man who had a gentle manner. Helen returned his smile without saying a word. They were so very young. At thirteen she was learning to be a wife. Frank, only a couple of years older, was just beginning to realize the weight of responsibilities of caring for his expectant wife and helping with the in-laws. Providing for the extended family was in keeping with the Navajo tradition.

She recalled laughing the first time Frank touched her bulging tummy to feel the movement inside. She had smiled as they lovingly felt the stirring of life together. They were both in awe of the miracle taking place in her adolescent body. Knowing love for the first time in their lives was part of the miracle.

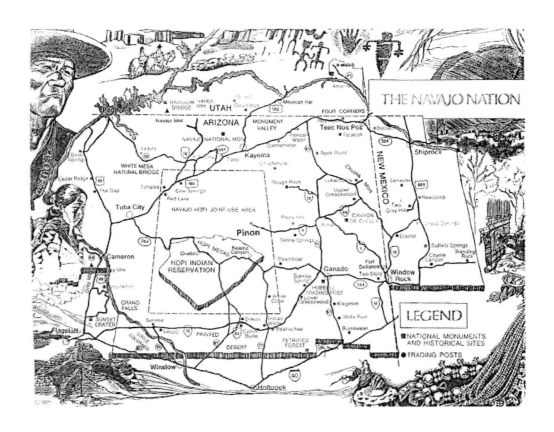

# MAP OF NAVAJO COUNTRY
## (Diné Bikéyah)
### SETTLEMENTS (some with original Navajo names)
website: navajonationmap

## Chapter 2: Helen and Frank

Helen's pregnancy rose high on her hips. Her medium framed body ached with the extra weight inside her. Her waist-long hair was like black silk threads tightly woven and twisted in a traditional bun on her head. She wore a beautiful turquoise and silver necklace with matching bracelet that was made by one of her uncles. As she let her hair down, she combed it with her fingers, letting it sway with the cool breeze of the day. Frank often gazed at his beautiful bride and treasured the moments together.

With no formal education and few opportunities for young Navajo men, Frank would soon have to leave the area and travel to California to work on the railroad. Time seemed to pass swiftly as Frank's departure drew near. In Helen's limited understanding, it seemed there was never enough money to go around. Although the pay was minimal, it would provide enough money to purchase necessities for his wife and family. He delighted in knowing that when he returned home, the groceries would be shared. The younger siblings in the hogan would fight over the fresh fruit, bananas, and soda pop.

Not only was Frank a railroad worker; he was also a **Roadman** for the Native American Church. He learned this trade from the Sioux and Cheyenne Indians of Montana and South Dakota. Frank was a religious man. He kept a sober mind, never using Peyote as a drug. He thought it should be sacred and used only for religious purposes. He had respect for religion. Frank would say, "Have respect for it; never let it go, no matter where you might be."

Helen watched Frank prepare for his trip. He neatly folded three colorful cotton shirts, an extra pair of pants, three pair of socks and several pairs of underwear. The clothing was placed neatly in a rawhide suitcase held together by leather straps and a buckle. He placed a photo of Helen on top of the clothing before closing the case. Helen was comforted in his promise to be back in time for the birth of their first child. Frank never mentioned it, but he was glad his bride lived with her family so that she wasn't alone while he traveled. Still, he knew California was a long way from Pinon, Arizona.

Growing up with extended family was part of the Navajo way. Helen had grown up in the home of Anna' Sani, her maternal grandmother. Her small world revolved around the Navajo matriarchal order. Traditional Navajo men tended sheep so the wolves or coyotes wouldn't attack and kill them; however, she sometimes found herself and her sisters taking duty as shepherdess. The shepherd life was not always easy. She slept on her horse in all type of weather with working guard dogs surrounding her. The dogs were definitely not family pets, and would attack strangers if commanded to do so. Daily the family would prepare a "**shepherd's plate**" for those tending sheep which consisted of mutton stew made from sheep meat, potatoes, carrots, onions and water along with Navajo fry bread or corn bread. Sometimes Mabel would sneak in some candy or chewing tobacco as a treat.

Helen also recalled the joy of learning from her mother, Mabel, how to weave blankets. In reality, it is the Navajo Spider Woman who teaches both young and old, as there is no "paint by number", and the only pattern to follow is what is in the heart of the weaver. Just as the spider weaves her

web of delicate design, so does the Navajo weaver create her traditional design. Learning to weave on a loom was easy for Helen. Her favorite was a "two-gray hill or storm pattern" blanket which could take over nine months to complete. The process began with caring for their sheep. Then the Navajo would shear the sheep for the wool, dye the wool, then card it into woolen spools of thread, and finally weave the pattern. The beauty of the finished work never failed to amaze even her.  One time, she sold her rug to a trading post for one-hundred dollars, which was good price at that time.

Even though Frank and Helen were newlyweds, she was glad to be living with her family.  Helen grew up living the traditional ways of the D'inah People (Navajo People).  Many of the traditions were followed without explanation.  This meant Frank was responsible to ensure the animals had enough feed and the family had enough food to carry over until his return.

Helen's thoughts quickly shifted to the fleeting moments that remained before Frank had to leave.  Lost in thought, she started combing her hair with her fingers, then braiding the strands into one long braid, unaware that Frank was mesmerized by her beauty. He sat and watched her every move as if he wanted a piece of memory to take with him.  Her hair was blue-black and shiny, flowing past her waistline.  Frank slipped up quietly, giving her a tender kiss and warm embrace before going out the door of their humble home.  Neither of them realized the trials that awaited them over the next few months.

## *Chapter 3: Travel to Keams Canyon*

The days in December seemed to pass quickly. Keshmish, the Navajo Christmas, had come and gone without celebration. It was Thursday, December 28, 1950, a true winter day. Helen opened the door to a pile of fluffy snow that had drifted next to the hogan. A rush of wind abruptly pulled the snow into the hogan and Helen quickly closed the door. Peering out the window, she could not see the path to the sheep pen or outhouse because the snow had wiped the paths clean. As Helen watched the snow fall, she was aware of the many changes taking place in her body. Her enlarged tummy was hidden behind several layers of clothing; one of which was a full three-tiered skirt of light blue calico print to keep her warm. Today was different somehow. She had a sense that something was wrong.

Helen felt exhausted and anxious because of the pregnancy, and she missed Frank. Mabel and her sister, Mary were engaged in conversation about family as Helen quietly listened to their chatter.

Suddenly, a jolting pain made her double over in distress. She wasn't ready for this type of pain. Then she felt a strange pressure building in her stomach and cried out for help. Auntie Mary came running to her side to see what had happened. She noticed that Helen's skirt was stained with bright red blood. Alarmed, she quickly helped Helen to the bed. She was concerned that Helen's water would break and she would give birth sooner than she should. Helen was only in her eighth month of pregnancy.

Mabel and Mary knew Frank was now in California. Helen's thoughts were running rampant not knowing what her body was doing to her. It did seem unfair that Frank was not there with her. This was not the way they imagined it would be. Then she felt another hard pain that took her breath away. She had to ask herself, was this baby getting ready to make an early entrance into the world?

She looked at Auntie Mary and questioned her condition in Navajo. "Auntie, what is happening…How can I do this on my own?" Helen, now beginning to panic, realized that she might have to give birth on her own. Suddenly, a wave of pain hit that was so excruciating she felt her own life go limp. She fainted.

It was dusk as the red skyline brilliantly stretched across the skies. Auntie Mary and Mabel hurriedly ran to the shed to ready the horse and wagon. It was snowing lightly, and the cold brisk wind didn't help matters as they pulled the wagon out of the shed. Auntie Mary thought to herself, "This is not the time to think slowly." The ride could take up to five hours in the mid-winter conditions, and the dirt roads could hardly be detected due to the deep fresh snow. The full moon's glow would help light their way. Both Auntie Mary and Mabel said their prayers, knowing the night would be a long one for all.

They harnessed the two horses and connected the wagon to the team. Helen climbed into the back of the wooden wagon with the help of her aunt. A couple of Navajo blankets were piled under her to soften the cold hard floor of the wagon. Mabel placed several wool blankets on her to help keep the cold away; the blankets were placed in such a way that it looked like she was wrapped in a sack. She tried to relax, while Auntie Mary carefully maneuvered the wagon on the dirt road. There was no time to get stuck in the mud and she had to avoid jolting Helen unnecessarily.

Snow flurries started to fall heavily, and the cold biting wind kept both Auntie Mary and Mabel alert. The nearest hospital was at Keams Canyon on the Hopi Indian Reservation approximately 35 miles south of Pinon.

Throughout the ride, Helen heard the crunching of the crusted snow and felt the wagon slide along the icy trail. The falling snow didn't make things better. Helen gazed up in the dark as the snow drifted about her. Through a small clearing in the sky, she could see a full moon glowing between the clouds. She closed her eyes and wished for an ordinary miracle to take her away from this place and time. Yet when she opened her eyes, she found herself in the same place.

It had only been two years ago when she was celebrating her Kinaalda, celebration of becoming a woman. Once that happens you are ready to marry. As snow continued to fall throughout the night she tried to make the best of the situation by lying quietly, drifting in and out of consciousness. Her only thoughts were for the safety of her baby.

## Chapter 4: Keams Canyon Hospital

The Keams Canyon Hospital was a small Adobe brick building that had eight beds for patients. Two doctors and several nurses were on staff. Many of the Navajo families traveled to this hospital rather than traveling a greater distance to Gallup, New Mexico.

When the wagon pulled up to the hospital, it was nearly eleven o'clock in the dark of night. They arrived just in time for a doctor and a nurse to take one look at her before rushing her into another room to give birth.

Helen couldn't understand the words they were speaking. She wanted so badly to hear Navajo but the nurse was a Hopi, and the white man whom she suspected was the doctor only spoke English. Once Helen had disappeared with the doctor and nurses, both Mary and Mabel left the hospital and waited outside in the wagon. Because of the tension between the Hopi and Navajo tribes at the time, they preferred to wait in the cold rather than share the warmth of the hospital.

As Helen lay on the cold hard birthing table, she felt helpless while the nurses rushed around to prepare her for the birth. Ten minutes before midnight on December 28, 1950, Helen cried out as the labor pains overwhelmed her. Oh how she wished Mabel and Auntie Mary were by her side; but they were not. She felt so alone with these strangers.

All of a sudden she breathed deep and pushed down with the labor that had been pressing on her and was somewhat relieved. Her womb gave up her first child… a daughter. As the umbilical cord was cut, she was distressed to see that her baby was no bigger than the cornhusk doll she had played with as a child. Her little one only weighed one and a half pounds and would have fit in the palm of her father's hand. Through happy tears, she smiled. She would name her Mary Margaret.

She breathed with a sigh and relaxed, only to feel similar pains come again. The white nurse held her hand in an attempt to calm her. She looked at the doctor and tried to speak, but it seemed her words were too faint to be audible. He glanced at her, then quickly proceeded to take little Mary Margaret and place her in a glass-like tube. Helen smiled as she heard her child's first cry. She was excited to know her baby girl was alive. She collapsed on the birthing table.

As the clock struck midnight, Helen felt another hard jolt of pain like before coming from her still somewhat enlarged stomach. Her breathing quickened and she cried out for help. Again the doctor came to her side and said something she couldn't understand. The doctor tried to communicate to Helen that she was about to give birth to a second child, but this time there were complications.

Helen noticed the doctor held some awful looking instrument in his hands and was moving toward her. The cold metal was placed between her legs and slipped inside her womb. She felt so uneasy and weak, she thought she was about to die. She was shocked and did not know what was about to happen when the doctor started to tug another tiny baby from within her. She could hardly bear the pain.

Helen screamed in agony as she pressed down to give birth, but the baby wasn't coming. She knew something was terribly wrong. The pain was excruciating. A Hopi nurse rushed to her side and gave her something that smelled awful. Seconds later, she realized in her semi-consciousness state that something had slipped from her womb. Her second child had arrived – another baby girl.

Astonished, Helen, glowed with excitement as she thought, "Who would have imagined giving birth to twins?" She beamed as she heard her little baby cry as the first baby had done. Her thoughts were of Frank and how delighted he would be to know she had given birth to twin babies. Among her people, twins were an honor. She couldn't wait to tell him the news, but that would have to wait. Now her body lay limp and her breathing became more relaxed.

This little one would be called Susan Rose. Helen closely watched every move of the doctor and nurse and noticed this baby was even smaller than little Mary Margaret. It was all too much for Helen as she collapsed in pain and relief. She was just happy to know she had twin babies, and both were alive. The doctor gave her some medicine, and she soon fell asleep on the table.

She woke the next morning with postpartum cramping from giving birth to twins. All she wanted was to see her babies, to have them in her arms, and to love them. But that wasn't to happen. Helen's experience as a new mother came crashing down. She wasn't allowed to see or hold her babies. She feared the worst. Her Navajo language was the only way she could communicate, and now she found herself so alone and afraid.

Helen was desperate to know what the doctors and nurses were saying, but all she was able to see were several people talking among themselves, ignoring her cries. Then a strange man dressed in a black suit approached her bedside and began speaking in English. He seemed to be impatient with her because she couldn't understand him. In actuality, the staff and doctor felt Helen was too young and did not understand her babies would need special care as they weighed much less than full-term babies. The doctor had to consider the infants' need to stay in the incubator until their organs could work on their own. The white doctor and man discussed the breathing problems due to the underdeveloped lungs, greater risk for life threatening infections, cerebral palsy, heart conditions, the possibility of learning disabilities and blindness. Although the doctor and nurses were discussing these risks, Helen didn't realize the seriousness of these conditions.

Then the doctor came to her bedside and asked her to do something. If only she could understand! A white paper was placed before her and a pencil was placed in her hand. He motioned to Helen to use the pencil and paper. She hadn't any formal education but was taught to make an "X" for her signature. Maybe the paper was about her babies. Whatever it was, she made an "X" on the paper.

Now the doctor demonstrated to her to place her thumb on the same white paper. This time he had a small bottle of black fluid ink and put her right thumb at the top of the bottle then tipped the bottle a little. Then he made her place her blackened thumb on the blank paper next to the "X." She quickly tried to wipe off the ink onto her hospital gown which left an ugly stain. Immediately the intimidating stranger took the paper from her and disappeared from the room.

Helen stayed in the hospital for one week without seeing or knowing what had happened to her babies. Each day she asked about her twins and each day the nurses would say something that she couldn't understand. All she knew was that they were alive. Their birth and infant cries were still vivid on her mind. She knew she saw and heard her babies cry; she had selected recognition. To the best of Helen's understanding, the hospital was a safe place where they would surely take care of her two little girls.

The day Helen was to return home with her twin girls, Auntie Mary and Mabel arrived. As she prepared to dress, she looked at the doctor in the doorway and asked in Navajo for her babies. He towered over her as he produced the white paper with her "X" and thumbprint on it. He issued a command in English which made her think he wanted her to comply. With his hand and facial expressions, she could only make out, "Come back in two months to pick up your babies."

She wrestled with this reasoning… surely they couldn't be asking her to leave her children? How could this be? She began to weep but was comforted by her mother and Auntie Mary. If only she knew what they were saying to her, but they made no sense at all. Whatever they were trying to tell her, she believed it was temporary and would be best for her babies.

As Helen, Mabel, and Auntie Mary began their lonely procession slowly down the road to home, she knew her babies were alive and well. Knowing that alone helped her deal with the reality of not having them with her. Although she didn't understand why this was happening, she had to trust the wisdom of the doctors. Her head was telling her to listen to the experts, but her mother's heart told her something else.

As soon as they arrived home, she went to bed without saying a word.

# Chapter 5: Postpartum Blues

Once home, she realized that her body still faced the challenges of the postpartum process. Her small breasts were enlarged and they ached. She wasn't sure what to do but her mother told her to retrieve watercress, wild cabbage leaves or other plant leaves that grew near the water. She placed the cool leaves onto her breasts which relieved the ache. Still, her body seemed to remind her of little Margaret and tiny baby Rose.

The days of the week passed quickly as she knew Frank would be arriving home from California soon. He would be excited to know she had delivered twin babies. What frightened her was how he would learn the babies were not home. She would just have to tell the truth.

She knew Frank was a kind and gentle man that had never yelled or hit her. Her anxiety was high and her eyes were red from crying each day since coming home. Pacing the floor of the small Hogan, she hoped this pain in her stomach would go away; but it didn't. Neither did the ache in her heart.

The day finally arrived when Frank would be coming home. She dreaded facing him. When Helen heard the wagon pulling up, she heard voices of several men speaking. She knew the time had come. Her thoughts were running wildly, if only Mabel or Auntie Mary could be here. It seemed everyone left her alone to speak with Frank. This was the worst part, being alone and telling Frank the news. She questioned herself, she replayed the scene in her mind… what would he say and what would he do?

As Frank opened the door he didn't receive the greeting he had been looking forward to. Instead, he saw his young bride with a look of anguish, her eyes red and swollen. Helen tried to avoid his questioning gaze and turned away. Frank took tentative steps toward her, as fear began to grip him. Finally, he turned her toward him forcing her to look into his eyes.

"Helen, what is wrong? Are you all right? Is it the baby? What has happened?"

Helen cried as she stated, "Oh Frank, why weren't you here with me?"

He pulled Helen into his chest and held her close as she told what had happened at the hospital. Frank held his breathe and tried to take it all in. He was a daddy now – a father of twin girls. As he consoled Helen, she knew how much he loved her. It was an unconditional love. She collapsed totally in his arms. They both wept together. Frank was relieved to know the babies were alive and well. Soon they would be reunited and this heart wrenching experience would be over.

## Chapter 6: Preparing for the Twins

To prepare for the twin babies, Helen made ready by purchasing two pink infant outfits from the Pinon Trading Post. Frank gave her $20.00 to purchase what she needed which included two baby bottles, cloth diapers, little socks, and two matching baby blankets. Knowing Mary Margaret and Susan Rose were tiny, she bought the smallest size. She would put them in the trunk at home until the twins arrived.

Now that Frank knew he had twin girls, he lovingly crafted two cradleboards from a secluded cedar tree. The wood could not have been struck by lightning, rubbed against by a bear, or broken by the wind as they are thought to be a gift from the Holy People. The backboards represent mother earth and father sky. Then Frank carved a small initial into each of the cradleboards.

Before leaving again to work on the Southern Pacific Railroad, Frank made sure that Helen had everything ready for the twins to come home. He never doubted that he would love and care for his twin girls and looked forward to seeing them on the next trip home.

The two months passed quickly, but not fast enough. Thoughts of her babies were on her mind every minute of the day. Helen was grateful to know she would bring her babies home and looked forward to seeing the smiles of her twins, Mary Margaret and Susan Rose. She knew that Frank would be happy to see the twins. She longed for the day that Frank would be there too and they could finally be together as a family.

The first day of March 1951 had finally arrived. Helen's special day had come. Frank was still in California, but she was excited for both of them. This day she would travel to the hospital and bring her babies home. Unlike the difficult journey she had made on that dark, cold night two months earlier; the thirty-five-mile wagon ride was not hard. This time the roads were clear of snow and mud. Mabel and Auntie Mary came with her to help care for the babies on the way home.

Once at the hospital, Helen passed through the familiar entrance. As she looked down the hall, she recognized the doctor who delivered the twins. He looked up and noticed her, too. He looked straight at her, but his face looked puzzled. He quickly came forward and pulled her into an empty room. A Hopi nurse followed close behind. Slipping his arm around her shoulder, he motioned for her to sit. He started to speak the only language he knew, English. She could tell he was trying to tell her something important, but his language was foreign to her. He knew it would be difficult to talk to her and make her understand what he had to tell her.

With his arm still around her shoulder, and holding her as if Helen was his daughter, he pulled her even closer to him. In a whispered voice, he said something very caring; still she couldn't understand. Helen only knew something was wrong, and she started to cry. Between the sobs and her strained voice, she wailed in Navajo, "Where are my babies?"

As she kept repeating through her tears, "Where are my babies?" Both the doctor and nurse knew from her cries she wanted her babies and she didn't want to leave without them. The Hopi nurse came forward, gave her a handkerchief, and tried, to no avail, to comfort the distraught young mother.

Helen turned toward Auntie Mary to see if she could help. But Auntie Mary only spoke Navajo also. Then Auntie Mary looked at the Hopi nurse and pleaded for her to help. The nurse shook her head and disappeared out the door leaving the door open as she moved quickly down the hallway. Helen appeared exhausted from her tears as the doctor sat holding her close. How unforgivable to loose both her babies. The room was filled with the muffled tears of both Auntie Mary and Helen.

A few minutes later, a young Navajo boy of about 20 years of age appeared in the doorway of the room. He promptly walked toward the white doctor and spoke both Hopi and English. The nurse reappeared and listened to what the doctor was telling the young boy. Helen could tell through the doctor's hand motion and the nurse pointing toward Helen that something had happened to her babies. She sat terrified and motionless. The boy then came toward her and Auntie Mary. He directed his conversation to Auntie Mary speaking in Navajo. Helen could tell he didn't want to look directly at her.

The young boy lowered his head and spoke in Navajo. "The doctor felt Helen couldn't take care of her babies because she was so young. She doesn't speak English; she can't read or write. The paper she signed with a thumbprint and "X" was for adoption. Her babies are already out of the area."

Helen's eyes swelled up even more and all she could do was wail. The tears now were streaming down her face and her whole body ached. She didn't want to believe what was happening to her. Her frustration upon realizing she had not even had the chance to touch or hold her babies – and now they were lost! In truth, she knew life's hardships, and this was one of the worst days of her young life. This day would forever change her destiny. At the age of thirteen, she was learning how life could be cruel. She just didn't know how cruel.

Helen's tears kept flowing and the knife-like pain penetrated her soul. It made her physically weak. She was angry with herself most of all. She blamed herself for the mistake. She thought, "How could this have happened? I've done something very wrong. How can I explain this to Frank?" Helen wanted to scream aloud at everyone around her, but all she could do was cry. All her tears did no good.

Auntie Mary now came over to Helen and pulled her close. As Helen tried to stand up, her body told her it wanted to fall to the ground and never get up, but she knew she had to keep going. All Helen wanted to do was get out of the hospital fast! Together Helen and Auntie Mary walked down the endless hallway to leave the hospital. As they left, Helen could hear the cry of a baby, but she knew it wasn't hers. It must belong to someone else. Helen also heard the doctor and the nurse's muffled cries as they tried to hold back their tears. She knew they felt the pain as well. It was too late to do anything now but go home.

Auntie Mary helped Helen climb into the wagon.  Then, sitting next to her, she drove in silence.  It was now raining, but Helen didn't care.  She wasn't taking her twin babies home.  She felt the rain on her face along with her tears.  To Helen, even Mother Earth felt her pain as it continued to rain throughout the day.  As they slowly drove the dirt road leaving the Keams Canyon area, Helen never looked back.  It seemed her whole world had crashed around her.  She wept all the way home.

## Chapter 7:  Frank Tsosie Comes Home

When Frank arrived home, he was delighted to find the Hogan warm and rushed to see the babies first thing.  To his surprise, he found no joyful sounds of babies crying – only silence.  Frank walked toward Helen, but she wouldn't look at him directly.  As she stood, she humbled herself before Frank.  He pulled her up to sit on the bedside.  Her eyes wet with tears, she told him everything that had happened when she went back to the hospital.  He gently cradled her in his arms, gave her a tender kiss, and said nothing for what seemed like ages. "The smart one will come home." he whispered. He believed that someday, one of the twins would find her way home.  They held each other tightly for a long time before Frank stood up and walked away, into the night to cry alone.

As Helen cried softly, she prayed in her heart to Mother Earth and Father God that her babies would be safe and well.  She blamed herself for the mistake that cost her  the twins.  She could not understand why, and wondered if she was being punished because of her lack of education.  All she knew was, somewhere her babies were crying for their mother, and she couldn't be there with them.  Oh if she had done something differently.  Tears came so easy, but they didn't take away the pain.  In fact, she never stopped crying for her babies, and never stopped praying that one day her lost babies would find their way home.  From that day forward, she was determined to have hope of finding little Mary Margaret and tiny baby Susan Rose.

# SECTION II

### *Chapter 8: Albert and Wilmont*

Albert was from Idaho.  Wilmont was from Utah.  They met while serving as missionaries for their church in Chicago, at Northern States Mission in 1928.  After both returned home, Albert age 25 and Wilmont age 30, married and moved to Idaho.  Their personal lives were different, yet they loved each other and wanted a family to continue their heritage.

In 1932, Wilmont was considered a city girl.  She was now married to Albert living on the "Lewis and Clark Trail" of Southern Idaho with few of the conveniences to which she was accustomed.  She referred to their small house as a "homestead shed."  She hated it!

The winds would blow through the wood framed house no matter what she tried to do to make it better. There was no inside plumbing, and the

Wilmont and Albert Johnson.  Living in Hyrum, Cache County, Utah in 1950.

outhouse seemed to be so far away, although it was only 40 feet from their house.  The only source of heat came from a wood heater.  They had an added feature with a cast iron cook stove.  A pile of wood was stacked against the back porch door; the wood had to be cut with an axe and then carried in.  During the winter, chopping wood was a chore Wilmont despised.

The one luxury Wilmont brought with her to Idaho was a 1932 Model T Ford.  Driving it, however, had restrictions.  She could drive the vehicle into Bancroft and Chesterfield Towns by giving a 24-hour notice.  Later she was told the automobile scared the horses.

The Chesterfield area was scenic as the open range of wheat fields provided a beautiful backdrop for their home. Wilmont loved standing waist high in the middle of the wheat field listening to the swaying grain. The backyard was the playground of the bear, deer, antelope, and elk.

Even though the land was beautiful, the harsh living conditions were challenging. One time a skunk got under the house. Albert crawled after him with a gun only to be sprayed in the eyes. It took several weeks to rid the family of the pungent smell.

Albert was a very capable "dirt farmer," as he cleared and seeded his own property. He was six feet tall – a sturdy built man weighing approximately 230 pounds. His hands told the story of years of hard work. He only had an eighth grade education, but drew from a wealth of experience as a dairyman, farmer, rancher, and gardener as well as a salesman. Albert kept detailed records of his various animals which included chickens, pigs, horses, milking cows, and dogs. He even gave names to each of his animals and knew each of their names by heart. He had a personal "who's who" photo album showing his favorite horses and milking cows.

Albert was creative with his hands as he made intricate 8-braided leather hackamores and bridles. He was a true wild western cowboy of 1930's and had a talent for breaking horses. By the age of thirty, he reluctantly gave up his horse breaking because of his many broken bones.

The Depression brought severe hardship for the people of Idaho – especially the farmers. Although the wealthy lost huge amounts of money, those who were already poor suffered as well. To add to the suffering, Wilmont lost her first born child, a girl named Shirley Kay, in 1933. Albert did the best he could, but it seemed that living in Idaho was too much for Wilmont. Neither one wrote or spoke of the years between 1933 and 1936.

Sunshine did come to both with the birth of a healthy baby boy in January of 1936. They named him Gordon. Still living in the Idaho wilderness, Wilmont hoped and dreamed that one day they could have more children. Then, in 1939 with the loss of a stillborn child, Wilmont stayed with her family in Ogden, Utah. After the burial of their child, she was able to return to Idaho. It seemed that all her hopes and dreams of having more children had ended. The doctors informed her that she could no longer have children. It would be hard to return to Idaho because she felt so alone in that remote and desolate area. She loved Albert and felt comforted by his love. Gordon was a bundle of joy that helped heal some of the pain of Idaho.

The Fredrick Albert Johnson Property, Chesterfield, Idaho,1999

## Chapter 9: Colliston, Utah

The time came when the decision was made to move to a small dry farm in Colliston, Utah. It wasn't Ogden where Wilmont grew up, but it was in Utah with no wildlife roaming in her backyard. This seemed to be a happier time for the Johnson family.

The Colliston dry farm was a great improvement over their Idaho location. Now their home was a four room abandoned school house made of stone. On the west side of the property, the Bear River cut a beautiful path. On the east side, the Union Pacific charged through on a daily basis. Surrounding the home was a small yard, with a wrought iron decorative fence. Most importantly of all… they finally had indoor plumbing and heat.

The kitchen was huge in comparison to the Idaho place. Wilmont made pretty shelf paper to fit each cupboard. Her most beautiful luxury in the house was a bathroom featuring a pearly white tub with claw feet. She finally owned a Maytag ringer washer which sat on the back porch. The first item on her decorating agenda was painting the cupboards "Irish green" to brighten up the place. She also wallpapered the kitchen with a colorful cherry wallpaper print. The floors were wood slats with tiny openings revealing the ground below. Later she would cover them with vinyl floor covering. There was much to do, but to her it was a dream home.

In back of the little home was a small mound of dirt that held an underground cellar. The shelves held Wilmont's homemade fruits and jellies. She particularly liked bottling quart size glass jars of tomatoes, peaches, pears, plums, and apricots. On the floor, she kept bushel baskets full of potatoes and apples of all kinds. A large canister of honey and beeswax could be found in this hidden underground storage vault that was padlocked for safety.

From the front yard of the old school house, the dominant feature was fifty small paned windows covering the entire entryway. The enclosed porch had two larger windows looking into the great room. One of Wilmont's stories retold many times was her determination to make a "great room." One day she took a sledge-hammer to the walls between two rooms. Albert came in and was concerned that she was about to take down a load-bearing wall. She wanted a great room and got one with Albert's help.

The Johnson family lived in Colliston approximately five years. Then, in 1945 they moved to Hyrum in Cache County, Utah. They kept the dry farm but lived in Hyrum while Gordon attended school.

Both Albert and Wilmont had hoped and dreamed they could have more children, but after the doctors told them it would not be possible, their vision turned to adoption. By that time, Gordon was fourteen years old. The truth was that because of their ages it would be difficult, if not impossible to adopt.

Disappointed, yet still hopeful, they had heard from a friend of the possibility of adopting an Indian child. It was a long shot, but Wilmont decided to write and find out more. She received a surprising letter stating that a Navajo Indian child was available, and if interested, they should put in an application for adoption.

The prospect of adopting an Indian child delighted the Johnson family. They submitted their application and prayed with real intent that if God wanted them to have more children that this would be the way. One month later, Wilmont received a letter stating that a baby girl was available, but the Johnsons' would have to travel to the Indian Reservation to receive her.

As Wilmont prepared to leave, she received a phone call from the adoption agency saying that twin girls were available and asked if the Johnsons wanted twins. They needed to make a quick decision. Surely this was what God wanted, so they sent an immediate response. "Yes!"

The Johnson family budget was for one baby. At the thought of twin babies, they found themselves eager and apprehensive. This would mean more food, clothing, and expense. Even though they lived comfortably, they still needed extra money for the babies. At the time, Albert was working two jobs; one as a dry farmer and the other as a shoe salesman at the JC Penney store. Wilmont did not work but could sew if needed. She decided to approach her father and tell him the news. They were adopting twin Navajo girls. He was very happy for them and offered to help financially.

Late in September 1951, Albert had responsibilities cutting hay and wheat. However, Wilmont was willing to go alone to pick up the twins herself. After arriving in Ogden and talking to her parents about the trip, her Mother, Francis, decided to travel with her. Together they would make ready for the babies on the bus.

The Utah summer heat was hot and dry when Wilmont and her mother pulled into the Greyhound bus depot in Ogden, Utah. Clarence, Wilmont's father, kissed Francis goodbye. Then, while kissing his daughter, he slipped a little more cash in her pocket to help them on the road. He knew Wilmont was ecstatic to pick up the twins. The ride would be 1-1/2 days on an uncomfortable bus traveling southward through Salt Lake City, St. George, and then on to the Navajo Indian Reservation to the final destination of Holbrook, Arizona.

The heat was stifling with no air conditioning on the bus. Sitting next to an open window, Wilmont tried to swat the flies coming in with all the dust and dirt and still somehow maintain her appearance. The nights were cooler, yet still dusty and dirty.

Source: http://www.angelfire.com/al/silverball/don.html

| <u>NAME</u> | <u>BIRTHDATE</u> | <u>BIRTHPLACE</u> |
|---|---|---|
| F. Albert Johnson | 11-23-07 | Hatch, Idaho |
| Wilmont Bell Nelson | 07-31-02 | Ogden, Utah |
| Gordon V. Johnson | 01-07-36 | Ogden, Utah |

<u>**PERSONAL INFORMATION:**</u>

Mr. and Mrs. Johnson were married 1-23-32 in Salt Lake City, Utah. They say their marriage has been a happy one from which they have gained many personal satisfaction.

Mrs. Johnson has given birth to three children, one of which died before and one shortly after their births.

Mrs. Johnson has completed one-year in college, has been on an LDS mission and is active in church at the present time. She seems to be in good health.

Mr. Johnson completed eight grade in school and has been self-employed as a farmer. He has also been on a mission for the LDS church and is now active in that church. He is in good health and is interested in adopting a child to take the place of his own child who is nearly grown up.

The Johnson's own a nine-room home which is well kept up both on the inside and outside. They own 195 acres of dry land and 115 acres of irrigated land, and milking some 22 head of cows. They thought their yearly income would be around $3,000.00.

The Johnson home is located in Hyrum, Utah, a community of some 1,800 people. The home is located about 6 blocks from the elementary school, the bus however, for this school stops in front of their house and picks up the other children, and the high school is 1-1/2 blocks from their home.

Their son, Gordon, is in full accord with the plans the parents are making to adopt a child.

<u>**EVALUATION:**</u>

This home can be recommended as a good prospective adoption home. The parents seem to be stable, well-adapted individuals who have a fine sense of responsibility toward children.

They have been married for almost 20 years, which leads one to feel that their marriage will probably endure until it is broken by death. This means security for any child particularly when the relationship between the parents is congenial and mutually satisfying.

The home itself is more than adequate from every conceivable standpoint as is the income and resources. Any child reared in this home would be encouraged in educational pursuits to achieve his potentialities. He would be given religious training in good stable environment.

These prospective adoptive parents have fine attitude toward Indian children and have been considerable thought to the cultural problems in rearing them in our community. We feel in other words, that the home is adequate in all respects and that the parents are qualified to provide the proper atmosphere for a child to grow in and make a good adjustment.

**Adoption paperwork submitted by the Johnson Family, 1950.**

## Chapter 10:  Trip to Arizona

On the ride they talked about life changes, and Wilmont wondered what it would be like raising two Navajo baby girls in a white society.  Yet, she felt God had directed her to this important event in their lives. Wilmont put her arm under her Mom's arm.  They held each other close and pondered the new life with twin Indian children.  Wilmont was glad that her Mom accompanied her to pick up her new babies.

Many hours passed as they traveled through the desert areas of Utah and Arizona.  As the bus hurriedly passed many Indian families, Wilmont closely watched the Indian people.  She noticed they either walked, or rode in buck wagons along the dirt roads.  She also noticed the people were very poor.  They passed small homes made out of dirt.  They were called "hogans" having only one door and one window.  The women wore long "squaw skirts" with beautiful velvet blouses.  They looked very clean, but sad.

The men wore blue jeans with white shirts and Indian jewelry on their wrists.  There were some Indians on the bus.  They seemed friendly, and smiled to Wilmont and her Mom, but with limited English they only nodded to say hello.  They sat quietly only speaking in Navajo and motioning with their lips in the direction they wanted the other to look. It was obvious; they were now in Indian Territory.

Wilmont and her Mom now were in the minority ones there on the bus. They became fully aware of this as the Indians stared at them. Wilmont noticed the little children played and laughed as any other children.  When she smiled at several children and they smiled back, she was delighted.

Although this journey had been difficult, it was easier to endure knowing that at the end, she would finally have her two little girls.  After much heartbreak and disappointment, she was about to receive a double blessing.

As they came into the Gallup Bus Station, they met a man there who directed them to Holbrook/Winslow area. They were exhausted from the ride, but excited. Once they arrived in Holbrook, they stayed at the missionary home where they met a Navajo lady. The young lady was clean, healthy, and spoke both English and Navajo. That night Wilmont dreamed that one day her girls would return as missionaries and help their own heritage.

Morning came quickly. The autumn air was brisk, and leaves were beginning to fall. Wilmont and Francis wore printed percale dresses with matching hats for this special occasion. They prepared themselves mentally and spiritually to meet the twins for the first time. It was going to be an exciting day for Wilmont and her Mom.

As they prepared to leave the mission home, they prayed that all would be well. A taxi drove them approximately 30 miles to the Judy Swenchkert home in the Winslow area. Wilmont's heart pounded as the car stopped. Her mother whispered, "Everything will be okay." The small home was made of earth colored adobe. The pavement to the front door was broken with tall weeds sprouting through the cracks. The yard was dirt with a small, broken white picket fence around it. There were no trees, but a small cactus bush blossomed next to the doorway. The wind picked up as they neared the door, causing a small dust storm that stirred the dirt in a twirl. It disappeared as quickly as it had come.

## Chapter 11:  Judy Schwenkert's Place


They stood at the door and knocked, and were soon greeted by Judy. She was friendly and welcomed them into her home.  Dressed in a full apron, she held a baby girl who was about 18 months old.  The baby's name was Dolly.  Wilmont shadowed Judy into the next room, but her eyes looked at the meager contents of the home.  She could tell Judy wasn't poor, but her hands had to be full with three small babies.  As the ladies entered a larger room, Judy put Dolly into a playpen on the wall opposite of two cribs – each held a baby.  Wilmont knew these babies had to be her new children.

As they walked closer to the two cribs her heart seemed to cease beating.  Through misty eyes, she first saw Mary Margaret. Wiggling and squirming, the baby looked through the crib slats and stared at them. No friendly smile was on her face, rather an inquisitive look – as if to say, "Who are you?"  Wilmont looked at the other crib. There was tiny Susan Rose. With arms extended, she smiled and looked as if she was saying, "Hurry, come pick me up!"  Wilmont needed no further invitation.  She bent over and tenderly lifted the petite, dark haired bundle that she had dreamed of holding. She was so small, weighing only nine pounds.  Francis picked up Mary Margaret and gave her a big kiss.  She weighed only thirteen pounds.  Both girls wore delicate silver-turquoise bracelets.

Judy continued sharing details as she passed baby bottles to Wilmont and Francis. Mary Margaret took the bottle eagerly.  Little Susan Rose gazed up at her new mom and sucked contentedly.  A tender moment was shared as they bonded for the first time.

Judy told about the health challenges faced by the twins because of their premature birth.  Both girls looked so small considering their age.  She loved the children and felt attached to them, but knew she couldn't adopt them herself.  She had nicknamed Mary Margaret "Madge," and Susan Rose, "Midge", short for midget, because she was so tiny.  At times she would take the three babies for a stroll in one baby buggy.  Often neighbors would look at the three and ask if they were triplets. She would just smile, thinking they did look somewhat alike, as they were all Navajo infants.

Wilmont and Francis stayed for one day watching and caring for the new infants. At one point of a conversation, Judy said that she was also caring for Dolly temporarily. Wilmont asked if she could adopt Dolly too. Judy said, Dolly was not to be adopted. She was entrusted with the care of Dolly Goldtooth, six months of age, while her mother was being treated at the hospital for Tuberculosis. Judy said the State of Arizona had asked her to help take care of small infants prior to adoption.

Both Judy and Wilmont realized it would be helpful to keep in touch, so they exchanged addresses and promised to write. As Judy said goodbye to Wilmont and her Mom she too prayed in her own way that all would be well with the Johnson family. From Judy's perspective, she really didn't know what would happen to the twin girls that she had cared for and loved over several months. Behind the closed door, she cried and hoped someday she would see the twins again or at least know what happened to them.

The long ride home on the bus became longer as now Wilmont had the twins. She was thankful her mother was there to help. Many of the Indian people stared at the "bilagoona shima"white mothers Wilmont and Frances, with a puzzled look. She wondered if perhaps they thought they were stealing the Navajo babies. It did look suspicious for two white women to have Indian babies traveling on a bus going somewhere off the reservation.

A sigh of relief came as they neared the St. George, Utah area. Wilmont was happy to be out of Indian Territory because of the looks the Indians gave them. Ironically, they now received stares from the white people looking at them with two Indian babies. It was an unusual sight for both cultures.

# Chapter 12: Returning to Utah

Wilmont's family awaited the designated arrival time at the Ogden bus depot. As mother and daughter stepped off the bus, both with babies in tow, Clarence took them in his arms. He stared at the little girls and wondered, "What caused Wilmont to bring these Indian babies home? They are so fragile." He thought she was crazy since he knew her arms were going to be full taking care of these little ones. But in his heart, he was delighted to be a new grandfather. Now Wilmont couldn't wait to get home to see Albert.

Albert received a phone call from Clarence saying that they were about to leave Ogden with the twins. It would be just an hour drive to Hyrum. Both Albert and Gordon waited expectantly outside their home for the car to pull into the driveway. Finally, they saw the car approaching. Albert could see Wilmont sitting in the back seat with a radiant smile, holding both babies. The car came to a halt and Clarence got out to open the door for Wilmont. With babies in her arms, she approached Albert. Their eyes met and she tried to hold back the tears. Gently Albert took both babies in his arms. He gazed at the little bundles with thick, black hair as they slept. After a moment he said, "Wilmont, they're so small." He prayed silently that the girls would be well and happy.

Gordon, being fourteen, just stared at the twins not knowing what on earth to do with his new sisters. They looked like fragile baby dolls. He gave each of the twins a small gift, a baby rattle, as a way to welcome them to the family. He knew this was going to be a new lifestyle with twin sisters.

The following day Wilmont, Albert and Gordon sat around the kitchen table to decide on names for the twins. They wanted "twin" names to rhyme with each other. As the babies were already named, the decision was to keep one of those names. So, Mary Margaret became Mary Annette Johnson, and Susan Rose became Rose Wyvette Johnson. At long last, Annette and Wyvette were finally home. It was September of 1951.

The twins became the first American Indian children adopted into a "Caucasian family" in Northern Utah. This created quite a stir in their mostly white, Mormon community.

When the twins received their first physical, the doctor was alarmed at their size and weight. Mary weighed 13 pounds and Rose weighed 9 pounds. Dr. Burgess told Wilmont, "Mrs. Johnson, these little Indian babies are so small; they are malnourished, especially this little one, Rose. She may never walk, and will probably always struggle with her health. You should have left them in Arizona."

Grandfather, Clarence Nelson with the twins, 1952

It was Wilmont's dream to bring these babies home, and she was determined to perform a miracle with or without the doctor's help. She went home and told her family what the doctor said. With their strong faith in God and the prayers of many, they purposed to do whatever was necessary to raise these little Indian babies.

Albert was a miracle worker as he held little Rose's life in his hands many times. Health was always a concern, and after coming into the Johnson family, she had many bouts of illness. Pneumonia was the worst, and he had to give her special prayers to make her well. Sometimes that was not enough, she still struggled to walk at the age of two. Many times Albert would exercise her legs to give them strength. Finally, Rose started to kick. After kicking, she started to hop. That's when Albert gave her the nickname of "Little Bunny."

Cousin Jeanine Hodason with the twins. 1952

The Johnsons knew it would take one year of supervised observation from the adoption agency before finalizing the legalities. Mr. Darley, the Social Worker would visit often. He was a well rounded man who always wore a business suit and hat. Sometimes little Rose would catch him sitting on a stool lost in watching the twins play. He made many notes in his writing book. Mr. Darley liked to pick up Rose and hold her on his knee; she was so little, like a doll with large black eyes staring back at him. She would wrap her arms around his neck and give him a little kiss.

The Johnson family became uniquely different than any other family in northern Utah, if not in the world. Being as such, the twins became Cache Valley celebrities without knowing it. Their little brown skins were a novelty, and people were kind and inquisitive. They were known as "The Johnson Twins."

After cod liver oil, vitamins, and nutrition, not to mention the loving care of a doting family, the twins began to thrive. During the first couple of years, clothing the twins was another concern as it seemed they grew out of their clothes each week. Many of the extended Nelson family helped clothe

the twins often with hand-me-downs from cousins.  Several outfits were alike, but usually Mary wore the color red and Rose wore the color blue.

In January 1952, the Courts of Utah declared the adoption legal.  As devoted Christians of the Mormon Church, the Johnsons took their twins to the LDS Temple for a special sealing – an ultimate gift of love.  On that day, Wilmont dressed both girls in beautiful white cotton dresses, with matching socks and shoes.  As they drove seven miles north to Logan, Albert and Wilmont rejoiced that their desires of having children had been fulfilled.  They lived their religion and believed without a doubt that God wanted all families to be together, not only in this life but in the eternities.  Being sealed would mean that from this day forward, Mary Annette Johnson and Rose Wyvette Johnson would become the Johnson twins forever and ever.

Top Left-Right: Rose Wyvette, age 18 months; 2-years; 3-years
Bottom: Left-Right: Mary Annette and Rose Wyvette, 1953 and 1954

Top-Bottom: Rose Wyvette and Mary Annette
The Johnson Twins, 1953/1954

# SECTION III

## *Chapter 13: Naming the Twins*

The twins attracted many onlookers from the community when out and about.  With matching "pixie hair cuts" Wilmont would hold her daughters' hands as they walked down the sidewalks or crossed the street.  People became fascinated; they would stop her in the middle of the street to ask questions about the twins.  Sometimes they would even ask to take a picture.  The girls would just smile from behind the brim of their sunbonnets, charming everyone they met.  Both loved to smile and laugh, which made people smile and laugh with them.

Albert worked as a JC Penney's shoe salesman for several years which provided the twins with a variety of shoes from the store.  They loved to visit Daddy at closing time, and they were mesmerized by a magical canister that zipped through a tube-like maze and disappeared into the ceiling.  Actually it was the depository receipt canister, much like the ones seen at the bank, traveling in the glass-vacuum tube from sales department to business office.

Throughout the early years, Wilmont was the Church chorister for both children and adults.  The girls had fun helping her teach the children new songs.  She would write the words in large letters on the back of discarded wallpaper.  Mary Annette and Rose would wrap their arms around her legs while she led the singing, not letting go until it was time to sit down.  Later Mary would play hymns on a piano in the same chapel.

Wilmont was a teacher and mentor throughout the twin's lives.  Her love would unlock the puzzle of learning.   In 1955, the Johnsons had their first "home computer."  It was a large blackboard on the wall.  Each week Wilmont scratched a new word along with the definition for the twins to memorize. She taught the multiplication tables and how to diagram sentences. The old blackboard held a wealth of knowledge throughout the school years.

But life wasn't all learning from the blackboard. One of the best family memories was an annual event. Taking a spring walk to the family pond, both twins learned early in life to respect nature and the animal kingdom. While they walked, Wilmont used the opportunity to teach important life lessons using the natural surroundings. Stories like, "The Big Red Ant," and "Grandma's Turtles," became favorites with the twins. When arriving at the family pond, the twins beheld pollywogs and a few catfish. Annette and Wyvette especially loved the baby ducks. They watched in amazement as the tiny little ducks obeyed their mom's calling quack.

Of course, having twins brought many adventures to the Johnson household, as the girls became somewhat inquisitive and mischievous. Wilmont was always teaching the finer things of life. When they were five years old, she taught them to type, play the piano, and sew.

The first real memory of Christmas was in 1955 when Santa Claus brought an old "Royal" manual typewriter. At first the keys felt cold, but with each stroke they seemed to warm up. They were covered with a thin cut yellow masking tape to help the girls memorize the keyboard. They learned from the best—their Mom's high school typing manual dated 1915. Every Friday there was a typing test. Mary and Rose competed for speed and accuracy. The kitchen timer was used to end the test with the loud ring of the bell! After the test, Wilmont would circle errors with a big red pen, then place the results in a book to show improvement over time.

Piano lessons were a must in the Johnson household. The twins were daily on the old family upright piano. Their little fingers could hardly reach an octave, but after years of practice, both twins could scale the keys with ease. Each morning had them practicing piano 30-45 minutes, then switching places and typing 30-45 minutes. This routine was practiced twice daily for 15 years.

At the tender age of 5, the twins were given a "Singer" treadle sewing machine by their parents. The machine was without electricity. Being twins, they found that if one would treadle faster the other could move the material faster. Well, one day Mary pressed the treadle faster and an accident ensued. Rose's finger was sewn down. Wilmont yelled to Albert, "Come Quickly!" He came on the run from the barn to find the situation was most concerning. Of course, Mary Annette had disappeared. He had to take apart the whole sewing machine in order to pull the needle out. As Rose held onto her Daddy tightly with tears running down her face, he said, "Oh, my Little Bunny, don't cry!" Well, Rose had to admit it hurt! But that experience didn't stop the twins from sewing.

One thing Wilmont taught both girls was how to make aprons and how to make their own underwear out of "used flour sacks." Rose was so happy when the flour sacks had a small print on them instead of just white cloth. Later in years, Wilmont's nickname was "Mrs. Mode O' Day" because she bought so much fabric to teach the neighborhood children to sew.

Throughout the twins' childhood, trips were made to the Logan City Library. To Rose, it was a museum of archives. Walking hand-in-hand up the large steps to the door that looked like the national archives, they opened the huge carved door to a wonderful world of exciting books! The fragrance of books was old and musty. This was where the twins learned to whisper! Picking out new books to take home seemed a little odd, as there were many books throughout their home.

Wilmont inspired the girls to love reading and hearing great literature. Twelve years on a daily basis, she would sit on her little green step stool and read to the twins at least 45 minutes. They listened intently as she read works such as Shakespeare, the Bible, Tom Sawyer, and Huckleberry Finn.

Gordon provided many hours of laughter as he loved playing tricks on the twins. At times, he hung out with the Darley, Brown and Savage boys who raced their tractors up and down the street by the South Cache High School and tried to escape the drill of Police Chief Mr. Elmer Lauritzen. The twins looked on intently as Mr. Lauritzen talked firmly to Wilmont or Albert, but after the lecture he would give a big smile and wink to them.

Mary Annette would follow Gordon everywhere like a little ghost. Later on, he took both girls to the Utah State University where he worked at the auto mechanic shop. To Rose it was like a large medical facility where Gordon wore a white coat. He had to be so intelligent to work on automobiles that were lifted high into the air.

More than ever, Rose loved Albert, her Daddy. He worked hard as a dry farmer, shoe salesman, sugar factory worker, and later as a gardener at Utah State University. She would follow him around going downstairs into his secret chamber where he made leather hackamores and bridles. The pungent smell of the lather he used to make the leather soft before braiding filled the air. He was a true master at work. Many times he would lift little Rose upon his knee and let her sit and watch him work his magic with leather.

The Johnson family had three houses while growing up. One in Hyrum, Cache Valley; another in Colliston, Box Elder County; and later on in years a small farm in Lewiston, Cache Valley, Utah. There were fond memories lived out in the Johnson homes. One home was called the "white house." It was a large two-story white home. This residence had a barn, chicken coop, large field for two horses named Black Fly and Spider, and milking cows. As the twins grew, they watched many chicks hatch under the glow of a warming lamp. The household had a favorite cat, Tordishell, who seemed to be perpetually nursing kittens. Plenty of cats came in from around the barn when Albert set out a bowl of warm milk.

When the twins were six, the family moved from the "white house," to the "red brick house" or "the old Peterson home," on Second East in Hyrum where the twins remained until graduating from high school.

The "white house" and "red house" properties had fruit trees. Wilmont also purchased bushels of fruit from the various vendors in the Brigham City area. She loved to bottle fruits during the summer season. The fruit room was filled with hundreds of bottles of plums, cherries, peaches, and apricots. She also bottled corn, tomatoes, and pickles. The bread-n-butter pickles and mustard pickles were the twins' favorite. Throughout the year, they would eat from that supply. They also cherished her homemade pies filled with the delicious fruits. Rose's favorite was the cherry pie. Albert's favorite was her mincemeat pie, but he always wondered why there was no meat in it.

One of Rose's least favorite memories as a teenager was trying to kill field mice while staying at the dry farm in Colliston. Albert had both twins take a shovel, enter the grain sheds, and kill the mice before the newly harvested grain was put in the shed. Many a time Rose threw the shovel at the field mouse and tried to hit it while jumping up and down and screaming aloud! Rose really didn't want to kill the mice, though she did actually kill several. Her Daddy was delighted that they even killed one or two, or at least knocked them unconscious so that they looked dead. Then they had to take each dead mouse out and put it into a gunnysack, which was another challenge. This was part of their annual duty of preparing the grain shed for new grain. Later the twins knew why he had so many cats around, but that didn't stop him from having the girls fulfill their duty clearing the grain sheds each year.

While at the Colliston place each year prior to the seeding, Albert had both of the twins walk the fields, hand-in-hand, picking up rocks and putting them on the large wooden hayrack while he drove the tractor. At any age, that was hard work – and hot! Both would wear large sombreros to shield them from the sun. By the end of the day they would be hot, dusty and very dirty. Forget about the 'child labor act,' they loved it because they were helping Daddy.

Mary Annette learned to drive the Case and Allis Chalmers tractors, and a large heavy "Caterpillar Crawler" because she was built larger than Rose. But Rose was small enough to help Daddy unclog the Gleaner combine harvester. She remembers getting itchy shaft all over her! Later she became allergic to the shaft dust, so she had to help inside with household duties. That's where Rose learned to cook big time.

On the dry farm in Colliston, the Bear River ran through the Johnson place. Often in the afternoon, the family would walk down a little dirt road to the river passing two small canals on their way. From this vantage point, the view of the valley was picturesque. At times they would see deer drinking from the Bear River. The changing seasons provided a postcard setting for the river that ran through the property.

The train rumbled through the area on a daily basis. The tracks were located just east or across a dirt road from the home. When the train blew its whistle, the girls would run to see how many cars were on the train and try to guess what was inside. Rose remembers her dad said he once worked for the railroad replacing old railroad ties.

During the summer months the Johnsons had farm hands to help. Most were students from Utah State University or local high school kids. They worked hard and ate a lot! They slept in sleeping bags on the freshly cut hay of the hayloft during the weekdays. After a long hard week of working for little pay, they returned home on the weekend.

Wilmont and Rose prepared small treats and drinks for the workers at the Colliston place each day. They loaded up a small child's wagon to take to the field for the workers. Kool-aid, Hire's Root beer, 7-Up, Orange Crush, and water disappeared very rapidly due to the summer's heat. Lunch time and dinner was another effort, as the young men ate beef and potatoes, hot dogs, stew, corn on the cob, homemade bread, cakes, and assorted homemade or store bought cookies. The young workers devoured the food as they rested within the shadows of the large "Theves Poplar trees."

The little farmhouse had eight towering trees lining the front yard to help keep the little house cool in the absence of air conditioning. The trees seemed to glimmer in the sunlight as the breeze rustled through the leaves. Although the students gave a full days work, they still found time to enjoy themselves. They could often be found swinging themselves from the hayloft rope, then falling on a soft bed of fresh hay. The workers thought of Mary Annette and Rose Wyvette as their sisters or even another farm hand as they worked side-by-side. Rose remembers two college boys who were getting married and asked Mrs. Johnson many questions about life. They viewed her as a pre-marital counselor.

The dry farm work in the fields was hard, yet Rose loved coming to Colliston because it was also a time to learn quilting. Wilmont had hundreds of cut-out fabric squares ready to sew and quilt. Each summer they finished at least seven large quilts. The squares were sewn together in a patchwork pattern: bonnet girl, fan, mixed-matched squares all came together beautifully. Then out came the quilting frames. The finalizing of each 'tie-quilt" was supervised by Wilmont. The twins each had their own needle and thread, and it became almost a contest to see who could do the most. Their hands would swiftly go in-and-out underneath and above the quilt material, then tie the knot at each section to keep the batting in place. Hours were spent talking, telling family stories, laughing, singing, and just having fun together.

During the winter months, these quilts kept all warm when Wilmont left the bedroom windows open for a "breath of fresh air," no matter the temperature. Sometimes the girls would have five blankets over them to keep warm. Obviously, they didn't know about electric blankets until much later in life, nor did they even think of closing the bedroom window. One of Wilmont's quilts is on display at the Chesterfield Museum in Chesterfield, Idaho to honor her memory of quilting.

DAIRY PRINCESSES from Hyrum who will be candidates in the county pageant to be held May 24 are Annette Johnson, Sherleen Buck, Nedra Allen, Cheryle Covert, Deby Wengreen and Wyvette Johnson.

# Chapter 14: Young Adulthood

The sisters learned early in life that work was important. They worked several summers picking beans for 2-1/2 cents a pound. It was hard work for little pay, but it helped cover the cost of school supplies and needed clothes for school. Many of their clothes were homemade. Designing and sewing their own clothes was something they enjoyed. While attending high school, both worked after hours in the school library restacking books and vacuuming; at lunch time they worked in the small school bookstore selling candy and other supplies. In 1969, at the age of 18 the girls participated in a beauty pageant for the Hyrum City Dairy Princess. This event was written up in the newspapers and gained them local fame.

Mary Annette and Rose Wyvette
Sky View H.S. Graduation
May 1969

Mrs. Johnson had certainly taught the girls to save their money and to contribute to their church by tithing ten percent. By the time Rose graduated from high school, she had a small savings account of four thousand dollars. After high school graduation the twins moved seven miles from the family home. Each moved into a different apartment unit, but literally only steps away from each other. Rose found a full-time position as a claims secretary for State Farm Insurance in Logan, Utah. Mary worked for Utah State University Center on campus. It was different not living at home, yet they did each save enough money to purchase a car – a Chevrolet Malibu for Rose and Nova for Mary. Even Albert and

Rose, 1969

Wilmont purchased a new Chevrolet Impala at the time of the girls' purchases.

The most significant change in their lives at that time was the love of Mary Annette and Tyrone Douglas Young. They met while Mary was working on USU campus. Doug was 1/16 Oglala Sioux and had a charismatic personality. He loved being Indian and was concerned that both twins had lost their identity by being adopted. He talked to both about finding out more about their heritage. It was the first time someone outside the Johnson household talked about being Indian and asked if they wanted to know who their natural parents were.

One spring break, Doug announced he wanted to visit his uncle living in Los Angeles, California. Rose accepted his invitation to join him and Mary for the ride. The two had never been to Los Angeles, and were excited to go. They met Doug's relatives and had a wonderful time at Disneyland. On the way home, Doug asked the girls if they wanted to know who their biological parents were. He had already found papers on the names of the twins'. Where and how he found this information will never be known. Both answered, "No, not at this time." He did tell them their parents' names were Frank and Helen Tsosie and later gave the Navajo census numbers to both girls. The subject was closed, never to be brought up again. Little did they know that this information would be crucial to their identity. Rose remembers, "We were at a crossroad in our lives. I wished we would have taken the time to visit Arizona, but we chose not to as we were not ready to take that step."

Mary Annette modeling at Utah State University event (1970)
Rose Wyvette and Mary Annette (1970)

**The Johnson Family – 1970**
Rose Wyvette, Wilmont, Albert, Mary Annette, and Gordon
Hyrum, Cache County, Utah

# Chapter 15:  College & First Mission

In 1972, Doug and Annette announced their
plans to marry.  He also accepted a scholarship from
Pennsylvania State University for his master's degree.
Shortly thereafter, Rose announced she would be
serving a full-time 18-month LDS mission in
California's North Mission. Doug and Annette moved
just after Rose's departure to California.  This would
now be the longest time they had been away from each
other, and in separate directions. They were both far
away from the small community where they grew up
in northern Utah.

One of the first experiences Rose had serving as
a missionary in California was touring the Indian areas
of the mission.  This included northern California from the Golden Gate
Bridge to the Oregon border and three-fourths of Nevada.  Upon her arrival
in Sacramento, President Terry greeted her warmly as she walked off the

College friends surprised Rose with a "Missionary Send-Off Party" at Maddox
Restaurant in Brigham City, Utah.  June 1972

plane. He said, "Sister Johnson, I'm so excited to see you. I have a wonderful plan for you and your companion, Sister Mary Rasmussen. I want both of you to travel the mission visiting the Indian people."

This would be Rose's first time living among the American Indian people, and she was excited. Because of her adoption into the "white society," Rose had not had the chance to be with her own people. She was delighted and anxious to have this opportunity.

One day, Sister Rasmussen and Sister Johnson traveled to the Round Valley, California area. The Indians lived in a small area near Willits. They arrived early one morning to visit several families. As they drove up to a home with a small picket fence surrounding the yard, Rose noticed a petite Indian woman sitting on the porch in a rocking chair just relaxing. When the woman saw the car pull up she looked at Rose, hesitated, then stopped rocking in her chair. Suddenly she was running toward our car. By the time Rose had gotten out of the car the woman was standing in front of her. With tears in the woman's eyes, she wrapped her arms around Rose and sobbed. Tears were running down her face as she pulled back to look again. To her astonishment, Rose was not the person she thought. She stepped back, wiped her tears from her face onto her dress and apologized. She said, "I'm sorry, I thought you were my daughter!"

The woman told of how her daughter had run away many years ago never to be seen or heard from again. When she saw a young Indian woman at first glance, she truly thought her daughter had returned. This woman loved her missing daughter and had hoped and dreamed that someday she would come home. Later, Rose learned that the woman's daughter did come home and there was much joy over her homecoming. This experience awakened her desire to know more about her birth family.

Working in the "Indian areas" was hard for Rose because it was the first time she had seen poverty, limited education, health, and welfare conditions that were alarming. After Round Valley, both sister missionaries traveled to Nevada. The area they visited did not like white people – especially the authorities. Rose heard and read stories of white people found trespassing in these areas that had been shot.

The reservation appeared desolate and unfriendly. A few homes were run down and looked abandoned. The day Sisters Johnson and Rasmussen visited, no one seemed to be home. The first door they knocked on was answered by a large, intoxicated Indian man. Opening the screen door part way, he said, "What do you want?" Rose started to speak. He reached out his hand and grabbed her by the neck. He proceeded to pull her into the living room. Rose lost her balance, making it impossible to regain control. The man started dragging her in the direction of the back room. He was very drunk and over-powering. His tight grip made it impossible for her to do anything. As the Indian man passed the sofa, he pointed to a woman who looked like she was passed out. He said, "There's my wife, she's asleep." Shocked at what she saw, she knew where he was headed... the bedroom.

Rose yelled, "Do something!"

Sister Rasmussen was standing on the porch, frozen in fear. Her mind couldn't believe what was happening.

Rose knew she had only seconds before she would be at the mercy of this stranger. Grasping at straws for anything to distract the perpetrator she screamed, "Show him the Bible!"

With a rush of adrenalin, Sister Rasmussen charged into the house, shoved the book into his face and shouted, "Go find your Bible!" His concentration was broken which caused him to lose his grip as he reached for the book.

Rose fell to her knees and literally crawled between his legs, then sprinted out the door. Looking over her shoulder, she could see that Sister Rasmussen was still in the house. Rose shouted, "Get out of there!"

She backed herself out the door and both ran as fast as they could while the inebriated giant followed closely behind. He lurched forward, almost catching Sister Rasmussen. Suddenly a truck pulled out in front of him and started honking. The noise stopped the man abruptly. The sister missionaries never looked back as they reached their car. They sped out of the area not caring if there was a speed limit or not. Only dust was the real evidence that the Sisters were there.

President Terry received an urgent call from the Sisters relaying the events that had transpired. He said, "Sisters, pack your bags and get out of there!" They left the area and never returned.

That didn't stop the Sisters as they continued their journey to other locations throughout the mission. Rose spent nine months in Novato, later transferring to Marysville, Sacramento, Reno, and back to Sacramento before leaving her mission. She returned to live in Utah and enrolled at Utah State University with a small scholarship from Manpower to earn her associate's degree in Office Administration.

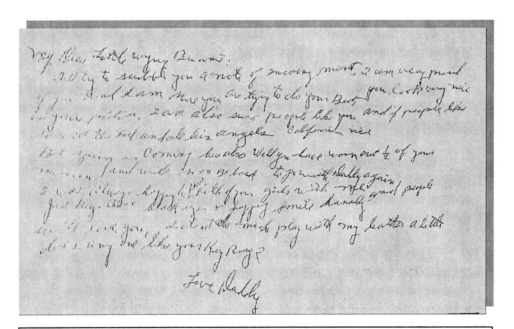

A cherished letter written by Daddy... "My Dear Little Wyvey Bunny:.I'll try to scribble you a note of merriment... Love Daddy (Received while on my California North Mission 1973) At this time he was diagnosed with Parkinson Disease, Diabetes, and Glaucoma.

Daddy (Albert) and Mom (Wilmont), at
the SLC Airport watching their
daughter Rose Wyvette leave for 18-
month mission, California North
Mission,June 1972.

Rose at Christmas, 1972, Novato, California
while serving a mission. Mary Annette made
the bathrobe as a gift.

# Chapter 16:  Doug & Mary with Desiree

Mary's husband, Doug, completed his schooling in Pennsylvania. Returning to Utah, he was well dressed and articulate. His charismatic personality inspired many Indian students to live their dream by earning a good education.

Mary moved back into the Johnson home as she awaited the arrival of their first child.  Many memories flooded back as she prepared for her first born in the same room the twins shared growing up.  Grandma's bassinet was retrieved from the storage room, and several of Wilmont's baby quilts were unpacked from the hope chest. Rose, who loved her twin sister, was excited that they were together again after several years apart.

Desiree Ann Young was born on June 23, 1974.  Her black hair almost overtook her small head, and yet Desi was a most beautiful baby.  To her mother Mary, she was a long awaited blessing.  Rose became "Aunt Rose." She loved the title and privilege of taking a child in her arms.  Doug loved both Annette and Desi, and it showed as he rushed downstairs to see his baby girl for the first time.

Nine months later on March 16, 1975 Doug's life ended due to a horrific auto accident.  Annette's life hung by a thread with injuries that changed her forever.  The local newspaper reported: "One person survives head-on… Canyon Collision Takes 3 Lives…"  In critical condition was Annette Johnson Young.  The newspaper showed photos of the accident of two vehicles crumbled together.  "The two cars collided with such force that it took two wreckers 45 minutes to pull the tangled cars apart." "Due to a high rate of speed, the car driven by a young boy failed to negotiate a curve, crossed the center line and collided with the eastbound vehicle driven by Young.  Mrs. Young was riding in the car with her husband."

Upon learning of this accident, Rose had to make various decisions that challenged her control.  Though she was emotionally distressed, she methodically made the necessary decisions.  Once at the hospital, her first thought was about Desi. Was she killed too? Moments later, the nurse said it was another passenger, a young boy, who was killed. The attending physician asked Rose to make a call to Doug's mother. At 2:00 A.M., she phoned Mrs. Young, telling her of the death of her only son. All she could do was scream, "No! No!" In her distress, she turned the phone over to her husband. Rose broke down crying too and had to hand the phone over to her roommate to tell the details. She was later asked by the staff to identify Doug's body. Crying uncontrollably, she had to admit that she couldn't. She turned to a colleague of Doug's and asked if he could handle the grim task.

She had to call the babysitter without alarming her and ask for her parents' phone number. She asked if they would take care of Desi for a couple of days. At the age of 24 years, Rose realized how fragile life can be. Annette was her twin sister, the only "blood" sister she had ever known. Now she was in critical condition in the intensive care unit and could die at any moment. All she wanted to do was crawl into bed and cradle her twin, but that wasn't possible. She couldn't even be in the room as Annette was being prepped for surgery. She was resigned not to leave the hospital. The only thing she could do was  pray and cry.

Ironically, Rose was supposed to have been with Doug and Annette. When asked to come with them to celebrate Doug's birthday at a restaurant in the canyon, she had declined due to prior plans to study at the campus library.

After calling her parents, Albert and Wilmont, Rose waited at the hospital with her college roommate, Debbie Harker. When they arrived, the family was able to lean on each other for comfort. The Johnsons were now in their seventies. Albert had failing health due to Parkinson Disease, Diabetes and partial blindness due to Glaucoma. As the Johnson family pulled together, they prayed. It was several days later that Albert gave Annette the news that Doug had passed away.

Fortunately Annette had wonderful assistance in making funeral arrangements by the ward church leaders. Rose helped by contacting and working with people who could help. Many students and faculty attended the funeral. An urgent call came to the mortuary where the funeral was being held alerting them that immediate surgery was needed for Annette. Albert, Wilmont and Rose left the funeral to be by her side.

After the funeral, Doug's body was flown to Pine Ridge, South Dakota for burial. During all the packing and taking care of the household belongings, the information about how and where Doug had gotten the names of the twins' natural parents was lost.

Rose shed many tears as she stood by Annette's bedside. She cared for Desi and brought her to visit Annette several times in the hospital. The recovery was long, but the love of the Johnsons and others supported her throughout the ordeal.

**Mary and Desiree Ann Young with Aunt Rose**
**Logan, Cache County, Utah**
**May 1975**

## Chapter 17:  Rose Finding Her Way Home

Due to complications from Parkinson Disease and Diabetes, Albert passed away in 1980.  The Daddy that Rose knew was no more.  The doctors had amputated both his legs, and he had gone blind.  At his time of death, he weighed less than 100 pounds.

Prior to his death, his children were called home for the last time.  Rose was living in the Washington DC area, and Mary had married a wonderful man, William Stanners Jr., and was living in Florida.  Upon seeing Rose Wyvette, Albert motioned her over to his bedside and whispered, "My little Bunny, I love you… do what you have to do to be happy."  Then he gave her a kiss.  Those were his last words spoken to Rose.  His funeral was held on Christmas Eve.

Wilmont passed away Thanksgiving, November 29, 1982.  She was 80 years of age.  Rose was visiting Gordon's home when she died due to 'quick pneumonia."  The marks of her life were those of a teacher and mentor.  Her life was her children.  She loved her God and knew if she believed and had faith that all would be well.  Most of all she wanted her twin daughters to be good examples, happy in life, and proud of their heritage.

Rose reflected on many cherished moments with the Johnsons.  She had learned to deal with life as a positive adventure that only she could accomplish . Throughout her younger years, she had fought death many times.  Her body was not as strong as her twin sister, but Wilmont's home remedies helped cure many illnesses. Pneumonia had taken a toll as she came close to death at least eight times before the age of ten.  But that hadn't stopped Rose from living life to the fullest… far beyond the roads of the Navajo Indian Reservation where she was born.

Rose lived in many states throughout America, first working as a secretary for a claims insurance company in her younger years, and later overseeing government contracts working with various American Indian organizations.  Her office and computer skills helped her throughout those years.  Not only did Rose have knowledge of the business world, she also had a talent for sewing and designing clothing for women that she credits Wilmont for developing.

In 1976, Rose received an associate degree from Utah State University, which was a short distance from where she grew up.  Later she continued her education at the University of Utah in Salt Lake City.  This young Navajo woman had become an entrepreneur – setting personal goals that only she could achieve…a living tribute to the Johnson name.

**Rose Tsosie Designs, Denver, Colorado, 1982**
Mary Stanners & Rose Tsosie
*The twins learned from the best...their Mom (Wilmont Johnson)*

Growing up a Navajo girl living in a white world was a saga of joy and yet silently she questioned her identity. Many times she was reminded that her birth was a miracle. Mary weighed about a 1-1/2 pounds, Rose weighed even less; both equaled out to 3 pounds together. Add to that the fact that it was 1950, and only primitive medical technology existed on the little reservation from which she came. God intended for her to live, and it was the Johnson's faith that made Rose healthier than ever before. The Johnson family provided love and care through her first twenty-one years. That seemed so many long ago.

While living in the Washington, DC area she consciously decided to follow the religious guidelines by which the Johnsons had lived because she wanted to, not because it was the "Johnson way." Rose visited various Indian reservations several times for government business and traveled throughout the area. The times she returned to the Navajo Reservation, she would scan the crowds, looking for a specific Navajo woman. Several time she asked herself, "Could this woman be my mother? Would I even be able to recognize the woman that gave me birth? Wouldn't that be a miracle?"

Moving to Colorado and becoming re-activated in church activities made a difference in her life. Could it be she was more Christian than ever before? She had to admit that two years in Colorado had made her more secure in what she wanted out of life. She had no way of knowing at that time, but there was a surprise around the corner that would challenge her "Christian thinking."

Her Bishop called asking her to come into the office and sit for a chat. "Hmm, sounds like he wants me to add to my church callings," She thought. Once in the chapel she noticed her Bishop waiting for her. He greeted her and asked her to sit in his office as he closed the door behind him.

"Sister Johnson, so you want to go on a mission?"

She answered, "Well, I already served a mission..."

No one realized that Rose always knew in her heart that another mission was in store for her. With a smile on his face, he said, "Sister Johnson, I didn't ask that."

"True," she replied. After several minutes of talking about this new adventure, Rose left his office with a smile on her face, knowing already what her answer would be. Later she called him on the phone. "Bishop, Yes, I'll go on another mission."

Rose's mission call was such that she had to depend on her own financial means. Her parents had supported her on the first mission in 1972. Now she needed to do this on her own. She decided to resign her perfectly good position with Council of Energy Resource Tribes that transferred her to Colorado in the first place. She realized many didn't understand why a person would drop everything they had and go on an eighteen month mission without pay to a location unknown.

To make this happen Rose sold everything she could. All her earthly possessions, including her clothing and vehicle had to go. She knew if she did her part, the Lord would provide the way. Later, Gordon helped with the finances when she was unable to cover all the expenses. Everything seemed to work out just as if she was meant to go serve on this mission.

Rose's secret desire was granted. The Church sent the "called to serve letter" announcing the destination and date of arrival to Gordon's address. When Gordon called, he said, "Rose, do you like cold weather?"

"Yes," she answered, pausing to hold her breath as she waited for the words to follow.

"Well, you have been called to the Arizona Holbrook Mission on the Navajo Reservation."

Rose shouted with enthusiasm! This would be her opportunity to learn more about her own people… the Navajo People, the Dine.' Gordon continued telling Rose of the specifics of the mission. Both were elated and excited to tell Mary Annette.

Mary Annette was married, living in Fort Lauderdale, Florida. Desiree was now eight years old. Mary Annette was excited for Rose, but thought her sister was crazy for dropping out of life to do missionary work at this time. Still, she knew Rose would do what she felt was best, and God would bless her. As Mary and Rose spoke, she decided to write Desi every week throughout her mission and hoped she would write a small note back. It would be a memorable journal for Desi to follow through her eighteen-month mission.

As Rose prepared for her mission, everything seemed to fall into place. Two weeks was spent at the Provo Missionary Training Center (MTC). Here she would be introduced to missionary guidelines for new missionaries. Many Elders and Sisters were taught various languages before going on to their destinations. Unfortunately, Sister Rose Johnson did not have the opportunity to learn Navajo. The Church evidently assumed she already knew the Navajo language.

The date came for Rose to travel south on the Greyhound Bus to Holbrook, Arizona. Rose was comforted to have three new Elders to accompany her on the journey. She tried to visualize Wilmont and her grandmother traveling the same road to pick the twins up some 33 years before. The travel was hot, but the bus was luxurious and had air conditioning – quite a contrast to the bus of 1951.

# Chapter 18: Mission Work

President and Sister Lynn stood at the door and greeted the "greenies" as the new missionaries were called. It was a delightful beginning with a lunch and gathering of various missionary leaders explaining the Arizona Holbrook missionary assignments. President Lynn had the inspiration and guidance to assign each missionary their location to serve.

Rose's first assignment was to teach at the Dilcon Boarding School, forty miles north of Winslow, Arizona. She would teach for nine months. This meant the sister missionaries would be responsible to teach a forty-five minute class on a weekly basis to the children. The lessons were about God, Jesus Christ and the Bible. At times, the class could hold up to 12 children attending. This mission was a chance for Rose to live and be among her own heritage, the Navajo People for the first time. The children and the elders were the ones to teach her the most about herself.

This was where she met Irene Begay. Irene was a humble and insightful Navajo woman in the Dilcon area. Her husband did not support her efforts in the so call "Mormon Church," yet every Sunday Irene would walk two miles to the church rain or shine. The Dilcon LDS Church was a double-wide trailer which sat next to the trading post. On a good Sunday, maybe ten individuals would show up. Sister Begay was dedicated, and ready to help with the needs of the church members in quiet ways. Rose admired and respected Irene's spiritual strength.

One Sunday while talking to the sister missionaries, Irene asked Rose, "Sister Johnson, do you know who you are?"

"Yes," was the reply.

Again she asked, "Seriously, Sister Johnson do you know who you are?

"Sister Begay, my name is Sister Rose Wyvette Johnson-Tsosie…" My mother's name is Helen Morgan and my father's name, Frank Tsosie."

Sister Begay inquired, "Do you want to know who you really are?"

Rose paused to consider her true feelings. Was she really ready to take this step? It was time to be honest with herself. Part of the reason she had taken this mission was the potential to learn more about her beginning – and possibly find her family.

Yes, was her answer.

Sister Begay was delighted. "Sister Johnson, I'll be glad to help you; my husband knows many people on the reservation." She left with a smile on her face and said she'd ask her husband for help.

Every Sunday the Navajo families would meet at church, but Sister Begay never said anything more about finding Rose's family. Six months passed. Then one evening Irene knocked on the missionary trailer door. She was exuberant and couldn't wait to tell Sister Johnson some exciting news. Once inside, she announced, "Sister Johnson, I found your family...your mother lives only 50 miles from here!"

Rose was washing dishes, her face a mask. She turned and calmly said, "Oh, that's nice, thank you."

Irene turned to Sister Thornton, who was Rose's companion now; and asked in a solemn tone, "Why isn't Sister Johnson happy to hear this news?"

Her companion explained. "You don't understand, Sister Johnson is very happy, but she has put aside her personal desires to complete her mission."

Rose knew that Sister Begay was disappointed with her reaction. In actuality, Rose was indeed ecstatic. For thirty-three years she had secretly hoped and dreamed that one day she would be able to find information on her own family. Now, before her stood a door that had been closed for many years. Now that the door was open, should she take a step forward or run away? She remembered years ago when her brother-in-law, Doug asked her if she wanted to meet her parents. At that time, she was not ready to take that step. That was eleven years ago. She dare not close the door on the opportunity God had set before her a second time.

The next question was hard to ask, "Would the Tsosie family accept Rose Johnson?" More importantly, "Would Rose accept them?" That seemed like a stupid question. Of course Rose would accept them. Yes, indeed, Sister Rose Johnson's whole soul was praying it would be right. Not even her companion knew the inner torment of the questions of meeting her natural family.

If only the Johnsons could be here to advise her. That wasn't possible. Still she remembered the stories that her mother told her when she was a little girl. She told the twins that the Indian people thought twins were a disgrace and would let the youngest one or smallest one die. That's why they put both babies up for adoption. Oh how Rose had hoped this was not true.

Rose had a deep respect for religion and growing up Mormon in the Johnson home. Somehow, she felt this respect and understanding would make things easier. It didn't. For the first time in her life, she felt alone.

That night Rose prayed like she had never prayed before. The prayer was simple, "God, if this is right, please let me know..."

As she continued, there was a warm feeling that flowed throughout her body. She felt God telling her in love, "Be of good cheer for I will lead you along... you are not alone." Wilmont always taught the twins to pray as if God was standing in front of them. As Rose pondered many things in her heart, she felt more blessed than ever before. She knew life's journey prepares those for greater experiences when we serve mankind. She hoped her service was not selfish and prayed that God would honor it.

That night Rose slept with a peaceful knowing. If it was meant to be, she might be able to meet Helen and her extended family. She knew Albert and Wilmont would be joyful with the news if they were still alive. The Johnson family always taught Rose to appreciate the Indian heritage. One day, while still living at home, Rose found a letter written by Wilmont. The letter implied that she hoped someday her Navajo twins would want to find their natural family and maybe even serve a mission to the Indian People.

# Chapter 19:  Rose & Helen

President Lynn appeared at the doorway and asked Sister Johnson to come into his office.  She followed him and sat down in a chair facing his desk.  He was a delightful man with a Santa Claus figure and a twinkle in his eye.  As a mission president, he had considerable insight for all the missionaries.  Sister Johnson respected his spiritual guidance, and he loved the Indian People.  He also cared for each missionary as his own child.  As both talked about mission experience, Rose expressed her growing love for the Navajo People.  She tried to explain to him that her desire to do the Lord's work came first.  President Lynn wanted to offer her a blessing.

Sister Johnson sat nervously in the chair as President Lynn came around the desk and stood behind her chair.  He placed his hands upon her head and started to give a blessing.  As he spoke, she knew God's inspiration would be felt and wanted to remember every word spoken. He admonished her to go with the Lord's blessing and said that she would go with a calmness she had never known before.

At that moment, Rose knew God was telling her, "It's time to go home!"  After the blessing, President Lynn turned and gave her a quick hug.  This was an emotional experience for both as they strongly felt the presence of the Spirit of God.

Sister Norma Ludlow, the chief cook at the mission home was Sister Johnson's companion for the day. This tall, sturdy built woman with a soft voice was  a wonderful chef.  Her husband took care of the missionary trailers and trucks. On this special day would travel some 40 miles north from the Holbrook mission office.  As she drove, Rose expressed her desire to complete her mission.  She reminded herself of the words her adopted mother often told her, "Do what the Lord wants, and He will bless you."

Once in Pinon, the Sisters met with Elder & Sister Blakemore who were instrumental in finding more details of Helen and the family.  When Rose wrote them and asked them if they knew of the "Helen Tsosie family" living in the Pinon area, they wrote back and said yes.  Then Sister Johnson learned later that the Tsosie name is common to the area, similar to Miller, Jones, or Brown among Caucasian people.

The Blakemores were directing their caravan beyond the black tarred roads of the highway.  The terrain was dirt washboard roads that seemed to weave toward small compounds or lead to nowhere.  To an outsider, the Reservation was like a third world nation within the middle of the United States.  But to Rose, it was home.

Finally at 5:30 p.m. the caravan of missionary blue and yellow Luv trucks arrived at the Pinon area where Helen lived.  As they neared the home there was no sign of anyone at the Hogan. Smoke coming from the chimney or a "chidi," a truck, just outside the door are typical signs that someone is home. They drove toward the home and stopped about fifteen feet from the front door. Only Brother Goldtooth and Rose got out of the truck to approach the door.

As she stepped out of the truck, she took a quick glimpse in the rear view mirror to check her appearance and thought, "Well, it's me.  I'm here, and that's okay."  She turned to look at Sister Ludlow who winked, smiled, and said, "Sister Johnson, good luck."  She took a deep breath knowing she couldn't turn back now.  A moment later they were standing directly in front of the door. They knocked and waited.  Within her heart, Rose pleaded silently that someone would open the door.

The door opened.  There stood a beautiful Navajo girl in her early twenties.  She had beautiful long black hair and a warm smile.

She said, "Yateeh," which means "hello" in Navajo.

She motioned for both strangers to come in, and they stood just inside the doorway.

"Is Helen Morgan-Tsosie at home?" Sister Johnson asked.

"No," was the reply.

Rose thought, "Oh no, we've come to the wrong home."

"Helen Morgan-Ben lives here." The girl answered, then inquired who they were.

"My name is Sister Johnson and this is Brother Goldtooth. We are visiting homes in the area and wanted to introduce ourselves to Helen. When will she be home?"

"Probably late tonight or tomorrow." The young woman replied.

Without invitation or announcement of their visit, they knew this could happen. Brother Goldtooth started a conversation in Navajo about his family and where he lived in the Jedito area of the reservation. As he spoke, Rose tried to listen but her eyes wondered throughout the small room. It was clean with a bookcase in the corner of the room. All she could do was stare at a photo on the top of the bookshelf. It was a picture of a young Navajo girl. The photo looked like her senior high yearbook picture. The girl's long hair was the only difference from her own photo

Rose couldn't believe someone else looked like her. Could this be a sister? As they talked a truck pulled up in front of the home and the girl said, "Oh, there's Mom now."

Rose swallowed deeply and turned toward the vehicle now pulling to a full stop. They excused themselves to walk out to the truck as the girl disappeared into the back room. It is customary that people within a house come outside to the vehicle to talk rather than the visitor coming to the door.

As Rose walked around the front of the large blue truck, she saw a Navajo man and woman sitting in the cab. Both of them turned and stared at the missionaries who had parked several feet away from the Hogan. The driver was a large built Navajo man with a wide brimmed hat. His eyes were cautious, yet warm. They were quietly conversing with each other in Navajo, probably asking, "Who are these people?"

Rose saw a gentle Navajo woman sitting in the passenger seat. Although she couldn't see her clearly because of the sunlight reflecting on the windshield, she could see the woman's hair was twisted in a traditional bun. She reached the passenger's side and the man and woman sat motionless – staring at her every move.

Finally, they stood before the woman who had rolled down the window about two-inches. Brother Goldtooth asked if she was Helen Morgan Tsosie-Ben. When she nodded her head, he started a one-way conversation in Navajo which lasted a minute – then total silence.

Rose turned to Brother Goldtooth, pleading with him, "Please, ask if she gave birth to twins at the Keams Canyon Hospital in December 1950. Rose understood the words he spoke, but she couldn't speak them herself.

Helen's eyes were moist with tears and she smiled the most precious smile that Rose had ever seen. No words needed to be spoken.

She quickly rolled the window down and pulled Rose as close to her as she could, holding her tightly. The only thing that stopped her from pulling Rose all the way into the cab was the door. Time stood still as both realized the magnitude of this moment. A miracle was happening before their very eyes.

All Rose knew was she wanted time to stop and for this moment to last forever. Her heart was pounding; yet outwardly she was calm. Within her heart all the joy she'd ever known came to this celebration of love. This was no ordinary miracle. Sister Rose Johnson-Tsosie had just met her natural mother for the first time in 33 years. Over and over in her mind, she kept repeating, "This is my mother. This is My Mother!"

At that moment she began to realize all the events that had come together for this reunion to take place. She knew now why she was meant to serve a mission in the Arizona Holbrook Mission. She knew why she was meant to meet Sister Irene Begay. She was meant to meet her natural mother today! God had divinely orchestrated these events in answer to the prayers of a twin Navajo woman looking for her mother and a mother whose enduring prayer had been to see her little girl again someday. Rose felt as if she was having a glimpse of Heaven.

All of a sudden, reality broke through with the sound of loud cheers from the missionaries who had been waiting patiently in their trucks. They watched the whole scene unfold. Some were standing in the bed of their trucks trying to get a full view of the mother-daughter reunion, many crying with shared joy.

Rose's initial reaction was of calmness, to her own surprise, but then she recalled President Lynn's blessing before traveling to Pinon, "...you'll go with calmness that you've never known before."

Helen then got out of the truck, she was wearing a red print cotton traditional skirt with a plain red velveteen blouse and white ankle socks with dark shoes. On her blouse was a huge turquoise broach with a matching bracelet. She was a larger built woman than Rose.

As she stepped away from the truck, she held Rose close, never letting go of her hand. Her eyes were transfixed as she seemed try to capture this moment in time. Helen then led Rose by the hand into the Hogan.

From the moment the two met, Helen was smiling with tears of happiness on her face. Yes, her baby daughter was alive, had grown up, and now had come home at last. Still holding Rose's hand, she guided her into the Hogan where she had been only a few moments ago. The same young girl stepped forward to meet her mother.

"This is your sister that has been lost – she has come home." Helen said in Navajo with a warm smile.

The girl rushed over to Rose without hesitation giving her a hug and starting to cry. Another girl came out from the back, then another girl, and then a brother... She met five brothers and three sisters. Rose thought, "Okay, I have to remember names," and she wished they all wore name tags.

Above Photo:"Red was the color of the day." The first time meeting some of the Morgan – Tsosie – Ben Family, March 1984.
Right Photo: Mabel walking to the Trading Post, 2002

The family was so happy to meet her. There were so many of them, and they were crying in joy. Soon, the whole room was filled with family and missionaries all talking at the same time. It was then that the Tsosie-Ben family confirmed that Rose was one of sixteen children. Wow!

One of Rose's newly met sisters insisted that she should meet her Grandma Mabel Morgan, Helen's mother. The missionaries decided to stay at Helen's home as several brothers walked with her approximately one city block down a small dirt road to the Hogan where Mabel lived. It was now dusk and Rose had a hard time seeing the path to walk, so she held onto one brother's arm. As she walked, her mind was trying to take in all that had just happened.

Mabel's home was a traditional hogan built with dirt and wood beams. The surprising scene behind the door was like a picture out of an Arizona Highways Magazine. A beautiful "soni," (older woman) was kneeling at a traditional Navajo rug. The warmth of the wood burning stove and the glow of the fire made her bronze face shine.

Mabel turned to look at the stranger in her doorway. Slowly, she gave a warm smile. Suddenly she arose and gave Rose a hug while tears streamed down her face. There was no need for an introduction; it seemed as if both already had met and known each other for many years. Rose was not just a granddaughter; she was the mirrored image of Mabel. Rose was a younger reflection of Mabel. This gentle Soni had gray hair woven in a traditional bun; her dress was a full three-tiered red skirt with a print top. She had a large turquoise broach on her blouse and matching bracelet on her wrist. If there was anyone else in the room, Rose didn't notice as she was hypnotized by her Grandma Mabel's warmth.

One of her new brothers spoke, breaking the spell of silence. In Navajo he told Mabel Roses' name and who she was. Her smile gleamed even brighter. As Rose only new English, and Mabel only knew Navajo they just stared at each other for a most precious moment of time. Rose knew then she belonged to this family. She shared so many physical features with the people surrounding her. She was a Tsosie and she now realized what she'll look like when she's older.

The brothers guided Rose back to the main house. Only moments later, she noticed Mabel had found her way to Helen's Hogan to join with family and missionaries all speaking at the same time – some in Navajo and some in English. When it was time for a "Kodak moment," the group laughed as all noticed Helen, Mabel and Rose were dressed in the same colors. Red was definitely the color for the day.

Meeting the first time at the Helen Ben Home, Pinon, Arizona – 1984
L-R: Grandmother, Mabel Morgan, Sister Rose Johnson-Tsosie, Mother, Helen Ben
Finding Helen – A Navajo Miracle (Not an ordinary miracle after 33 years of lost time)

## *Chapter 20: Meeting the Family*

During the next couple hours, Rose visited with most all the family named Morgan, Tsosie and Ben. Several stories unfolded about Frank Tsosie, her natural father who had died in January 1958 or 1959. Frank had finished working on the railroad in California. He was heading home when he froze to death. Navajo tradition prevents talking about the dead, so Rose was unable to receive more details. One of Rose's newly found sisters, Louise, did tell her that four men who knew Frank wrapped him in a turquoise, red and green printed man's shawl for his funeral. He was later buried in the Pinon Presbyterian Church Cemetery. His unmarked burial site is known to those that attended his funeral. Helen later married Bahe Ben.

The First Gathering, March 17, 1984 – Dilcon, Arizona
Mabel Morgan, Helen Tsosie Ben, Rose and Bahe Ben with Siblings and Extended Family

As Rose cheerfully talked about her missionary life, she almost forgot the special present she had tucked into her pocket for Helen. As Helen spoke only Navajo, Rose spoke through one of her newly met sisters. Rose was a humble missionary but wanted to Helen to have a special gift. She presented the gift that she had lovingly wrapped earlier that day. Helen was like a little child as she anxiously awaited the Navajo interpretation. Rose could sense her curiosity as Helen held the small package in her hands. Rose watched each move so she would always remember Helen's reaction to the gift. Helen's eyes were already wet with tears. She found herself wiping them away as she was trying to open the gift.

Helen awkwardly opened the wrapped gift; surprise shone on her face as she saw a photo of a woman and a young girl. She stared at the images before her. Lovingly she touched the glass protecting the photos, then started to cry. She turned to one of the sisters and with a look of hopeful anticipation, she asked, "Who is this?"

Rose could sense she was battling with hope and fear… could it be, the other lost baby? She looked at her and choked back a lump in her own throat, while saying, "This is your first daughter, my twin sister, Mary Annette and her daughter, Desiree Ann."

Suddenly, there was a rush of excitement in the room, as everyone began speaking in their native tongue. It was a joyful milieu as Helen held the picture tightly not wanting anyone to touch it. She wept as she stroked the photo of Mary Annette, knowing that her first baby was alive, healthy, and all grown up with a daughter of her own.

Everyone wanted to see the photos and hear about how "the twins" grew up together and what the other twin was like. Rose couldn't speak fast enough.  There was so much to tell.  At one point in the conversation a sister said they all knew the story of the "lost twins" and a search had been going on for many years.  They said Louise, who lived in Phoenix, tried to find help in locating the twins without success.

Time seemed to accelerate as they talked by the wood burning stove.  Rose was enriched to hear stories of the family.  There was much to learn about Helen's life.  She had six births at home in her Hogan.  Rose didn't know for sure, but believed she was scared to go to a hospital again in fear of her babies being lost again.  Rose thought of the many hardships her Navajo family must have experienced living on the reservation in the early 1950's.  Helen's home still didn't have running water or electricity.  Rose asked about Bahe who had disappeared. Someone said, "Oh, he's around." He was relieved to have Helen so happy.

Rose learned that Bahe Ben had tried many years to help his wife find information about her lost twins before he had finally given up hope.  The day Rose drove to meet the family for the first time, Bahe and Helen were on their way to Chinle, Window Rock to find the white piece of paper with the thumb print and "X."  It seemed like a lost cause.  Helen knew that if no information was to be found, Bahe would not help her again.  That very afternoon, Bahe and Helen had traveled about 20-miles from their home when something in her heart told her to go home immediately!  Again, she knew if she turned around and went home Bahe would not take her again, but the feeling was insistant. She listened to her heart, and that's when Rose was literally standing at Helen's door.

Rose's heart was full of love and she wanted to stay longer, but the time was getting late.  All the missionaries had to leave the Reservation before it got too dark because of the unfamiliar dirt roads.  Before everyone left, all knelt down in prayer to give thanks to God for giving them the reunion and answering everyone's prayers.

The ride to the mission home seemed short.  Rose felt like the little Luv Truck was one of God's chariots carrying them home safely.  Sister Ludlow and  Rose arrived around 11:00 p.m. President Lynn peaked his head out of the mission residence home and said he knew all went well, as if he already knew the outcome.  He said he'd like to talk in the morning.  Rose went to straight to her room to pray and cry.

This day, Rose was able to touch the face of her mother, Helen Morgan Tsosie-Ben.  Yateeh Shima Nizohnnee, "Hello beautiful mother." She couldn't wait to tell Mary Annette.

# Children of Helen

| # | | |
|---|---|---|
| 1 | Mary Annette Johnson, (twin), 1950, Keams Canyon, Navajo | Frank Tsosie |
| 2 | Rose Wyvette Johnson (twin), 1950, Keams Canyon, Navajo | Frank Tsosie |
| 3 | Louise Tsosie, 1952, Pinon, Navajo (Homebirth) | Frank Tsosie |
| 4 | Paul Tsosie, 1954, Pinon, Navajo (Homebirth) | Frank Tsosie |
| 5 | Juanita Tsosie, 1956, Pinon, Navajo (Homebirth) | Frank Tsosie |
| 6 | Esther Tsosie, 1957, Pinon, Navajo (Homebirth) | Frank Tsosie |
| 7 | Lorraine Tsosie, 1959, Keams Canyon, Navajo | Frank Tsosie |
| 8 | Boyd Chee (D.A.B.), Pinon, Navajo (Homebirth) | Mr. Chee |
| 9 | Wilson Chee, 1964, Ganado, Navajo | Mr. Chee |
| 10 | Franklin Ben (D.A.B), Pinon, Navajo (Homebirth) | Bahe Ben |
| 11 | Francis Ben, 1966, Ganado, Navajo | Bahe Ben |
| 12 | Evelyn Ben, 1967, Ganado, Navajo | Bahe Ben |
| 13 | Lawrence Ben, 1969, Chinle, Navajo | Bahe Ben |
| 14 | Levi Ben, 1970, Keams Canyon, Navajo | Bahe Ben |
| 15 | Allison Ben, 1973, Fort Defiance, Navajo | Bahe Ben |
| 16 | Benjamin Ben, 1975, Ganado, Navajo | Bahe Ben |

Letter from Louise Tsosie
Dated March 11, 1984


TESTIMONY:

I would like to bare my testimony on behalf of our natural sister, Rose W. Johnson-Tsosie [my older sister]. It's a greatest thing ever happened. I was surprised to receive a letter from my mother. I was astonished to hear our sister Rose came around back home at Pinon area. Oh Thank God! I was so humbled with tears and I gave the picture a great hug. And, I just couldn't settle down, wanting to leave right that very moment.

I never known we had twin sisters, until I was 18 years old, my Mom mentioned one day. Louise, did you know you have two older sisters, twins? I answered, "no." She went on and told me she had them at Keams Canyon Hospital. They was premature which both were kept in an incubator. At that time all staff at the hospital were nothing but Anglos and Hopi and she (Mom) did not have anyone to interpret for her and especially she's uneducated. She said that it made it hard for her and she didn't do it on purpose. One Hopi lady tried to interpret but it mostly by hand motion and she missed understood the lady. She was told to put her thumb print on the paper and she did. She didn't know it was for adoption.

She thought she was told to come back two months to pick up the babies; and two months later she went back to Keams Canyon Hospital to pick up the babies. This time she had (Auntie) Mary Kathy Tsosie to interpret for her. There they had found out she (my Mom) had adopted [out] the babies, which she was very astonished and cried for her babies. But the crying didn't do any good. No choice the babies were already taken somewhere. Since then she never sleep or eat food for some months.

I recall Mom often talking about our sisters in tears, she has always wondered where they might be, how big they are. Are they married or not. If they are being told they are adopted, etc. The first of last year I have often talked about them too. Wanting to find out where they live and who's adopted them. I wanted to investigate through special agencies or private lawyer at Tuba City, at the time I used to live at Tuba City, Arizona.

It's a great pleasure to find out we do have a sister on a mission which none of us never had. But we are a member of the Church of Jesus Christ of Latter-day Saints too.

Amen, Louise Tsosie (Sister)

Phoenix, Arizona

# SECTION IV

## *Chapter 21: Helen*

On January 9, 2007, Rose received a frantic phone call from Aletha Tsosie, Louise's daughter, stating that Grandma Helen had passed away. She tried calling several brothers and sisters without success before finally connecting with Paul, her oldest brother. He confirmed that Helen Ben had passed away around 10:30 p.m. in a Phoenix hospital.

When dealing with death, each individual has a personal way of coping. All eventually have to come to the realization that their loved one is gone from this world. Truly, Helen was a quiet hero to Rose. Part of her way of managing her emotions was to reflect over the accomplishments of her exceptional mother.

Helen was born December 5, 1936. Her parents were Mabel Morgan and Dan Morgan, both deceased. Helen married Frank Tsosie at the age of 12, married Mr. Chee after Frank died, and then married Bahe Ben, enjoying 41 years of marriage. Helen was mother to 16 children, grandmother to 64 grandchildren, and great-grandmother to 42 great-grandchildren for a total of 122 offspring. She was known as a Navajo Rug Weaver.

Since meeting Helen in March 1984, Rose was only able to visit her 10-12 times over 23 years. The time was too short, the visits too few. Rose knew one day she would have to deal with her death, but hoped that it would be much later in life. In her memory, Helen was young in 1984, only 48 years of age, and would now remain that way indefinitely. Rose realized visiting the family home would be different after the funeral because Helen would no longer be there; and if the Navajo tradition was honored, there would be no talk of her or photos shown.

As Rose packed for the trip home, she reflected on her love for her natural mother, the one who gave her birth.

One time Helen decided she wanted to know where Rose lived in the great Salt Lake City area, so she told one of her sons to drive her up to see her. She was surprised when he called and said,

"Mom wants to see you."

"I can come down in a month or so." Rose said.

He then said, "No, Mom is here in Salt Lake City and wants to see you now!"

Rose hurried out to meet Helen. Her brother said she wanted to see where Rose lived. The one-hour visit concluded with a tour of Rose's two bedroom apartment in Bountiful, Utah. Helen was happy with what she saw then said, "Let's go." Just before they left, Rose called Gordon. Both he and Lydia were able to meet Helen for the first time.

While waiting for Gordon, Helen looked around at Bountiful hills filled with large homes. She spoke in Navajo to Rose, "You can be only in one room at a time." Rose had to admit it is true. Helen lived in a simple hogan, raised fourteen children, and helped raise grandchildren and great-grandchildren simply. She was happy in her life, and that's what made a difference in Rose's life. We have so much and want so much — maybe too much for our own good.

Helen's death would bring final rest to her after years of life's hardships and challenges. She would be reunited with Frank, Mabel, and her two babies that died at birth. Rose believed that the Johnson family would be there to cheer and welcome her to the Heavenly home too.

The logistics to travel 400 plus mile to the Navajo reservation by vehicle was made possible through two friends, Lori Wiscombe and Lynda Christensen. Lori would be the only driver for the 7 hour journey. Their adventure would be taking them east toward Price with a scenic view of mountains, then 200 miles toward the land of the dinosaur area to Manti. Then they would head south for another 160 miles entering the Navajo Indian Reservation. Once over the Arizona border, they would travel 70 miles, with a final destination of Chinle, Arizona. Lynda provided a "gift basket" with plenty of snacks, drinks, food and some gas money for the journey home. Her thoughtfulness helped to make the long ride more enjoyable.

The January weather with snow and cold didn't stop the two traveling the distance without a map; Rose knew by heart the direction home. Once on the Navajo Indian Reservation Rose felt she was in her home territory. Navajo land was such a beautiful place to visit because of canyon lands and the various rocks glowing brilliantly red at sunset. She cherished the trips to visit Helen and the family. Now saying good-bye to Helen would be unforgettable, too.

On Saturday, January 13, 2007, Lori prepared her white Jeep Cherokee early to travel to Pinon. A light snow had fallen throughout the night leaving the Chinle area cold and white. Rose prayed that their travels would be safe. They would drive sixty miles west of Chinle to Pinon, passing through the Black Mountain area. Pinon is on the rim of the JUA (Joint Use Area) of the Navajo-Hopi Reservation. Helen had lived most of her life here and now would be laid to rest in the most remote area of the Indian reservation.

As they passed the Black Mountain area, Rose remembered on one visit when Helen and Wilson, her brother, accompanied them on a drive throughout this part of the reservation. They told her stories of the Navajo Way of life as Wilson interpreted. Helen wanted her daughter to have insight into the Navajo traditions and way of life.

Helen shared about the birth of her babies and what she did for her children. Specifically, after each child was born, she asked the doctor or midwife to save the placenta and umbilical cord. Each time, she would place the placenta on a cider, sage bush, or pinon tree to give thanks to God and Mother Nature for this child. She would bury the placenta in a special place for that particular child. If she felt that child was to have education, she would bury the placenta near a school; or if the child was to become spiritual, she would bury the placenta near a church. Each child was special as she kept the tradition sacred. Rose didn't know why she remembered this now, but she recalled the trip and how much Helen wanted to pass on this heritage to her daughter.

Rose told of one visit when Helen sat down on her bed and pulled out a trunk full of memorabilia. She opened a large envelope filled with pages of high school pictures. She nodded to Louise to tell the story of each child's photo. Helen smiled as Louise told of her brother Paul being a drummer while in high school. Several of the "Ben" children were good with horses and won several ribbons and trophies with the rodeo. Helen watched and listened, then pointed with her lips; a signal to look 'over there.' Louise knew what she wanted to say with only a few Navajo words. Rose was fascinated that all Helen's children were educated at a boarding school near Pinon or Chinle. Several young children were placed out in government schools in California, Pennsylvania, and Washington.

Louise told of when she was placed in the "Dillard" home in Pennsylvania. Mrs. Dillard spent many dollars helping Louise look civilized. She bought her beautiful dresses and shoes to wear. Louise was not ready to wear shoes like those given to her… they were too pretty to wear. Then she got homesick. She cried for her mother and Mrs. Dillard didn't know what to do. Finally after a six-month stay, Mrs. Dillard sent Louise home on the train to Phoenix and then on a bus back to Pinon. But before she left, the Dillard's purchased many gifts for the family. She heard from the Dillard family for several years… then nothing. Louise thought Mrs. Dillard was a nice lady with a large mansion and had much to eat.

Rose and Lori continued over the icy roads. Black ice had caused several vehicles to slip off the road. They didn't stop because they didn't want to be late, and they knew the Navajo Police would be out and about. Five minutes later the Navajo Police, in their white suburban, passed them going in the opposite direction. The snow had let up some, but it was freezing cold. Because of the blowing snow and fog, they drove only 10 miles per hour in some areas. Anyone traveling the reservation roads had to watch out for animals as well. The horses, sheep, and cattle roamed freely all over the area.

They passed the time by telling stories. Rose held Lori captive as she drove; she was a true Navajo storyteller sharing her many stories of the reservation. She told of how Benjamin won a 9-hole game playing on the Pinon Desert Golf Course. Rose's brothers liked to golf on the desert floors. First, one of the "Ben" brothers purchased a carton of neon orange balls. They would take turns hitting the ball for the longest drive, or see who could hit a hole-in-one; they would set up a white flag some 250 feet out in the desert somewhere. Avoiding sand dunes was a challenge, and if the ball got lost, there was a search and rescue for one little ball. The fact was they couldn't afford losing very many balls.

Another memory was hearing stories of Mabel walking every day to the Pinon Trading Post to pick up her mail. When the weather was bad she would wait by the roadside for a ride. She walked the five-mile trip each way on good days. Rose was amazed at her stamina

Rose and Lori made it to the Pinon area only a few minutes prior to the funeral, stopping at the Catholic Church as a casket was being carried into the chapel. Rose wasn't sure if there was a change in plans so they stopped to check. It was not her mother. Rose later found out that the person who had died was a distant relative.

The church was a small brick building that resembled a LDS seminary. Rose received a warm welcome in the arms of some brothers. Then she came upon Emma, her brother Levi's wife. She was so warm and considerate. Emma and Levi had been so kind to Rose since she had found Helen. Emma took Rose's arm and led her into the chapel to sit next to Louise and other family members.

Rose scanned the room to see who she recognized. Bahe and the pallbearers were in the first and second rows. Several aunts and uncles were seated on the left side, and other family members were scattered throughout the room. Many were craning their necks to see this stranger coming to the funeral. Most of the families had heard the story of Helen's lost babies. They were surprised to see one of the twins sitting among them. Brother Wintch was preparing to conduct the meeting.

While she waited, Rose thought of all her visits home and of the conditions in which Helen live for most of her life. It was a life of poverty and hardship. Many of the family had no running water and no electricity. The limited storage in their Hogans discouraged stock-piling groceries. Still she recalled every visit bringing a load of groceries from the Chinle store. A large layer cake with colorful frosting decorating the top was a favorite surprise. Flour, sugar, salt, and other basics like eggs, milk, bread, meats, vegetables were loaded on the truck, too. Several times when traveling through the Green River area, Rose would pick up watermelon and cantaloupe—as good as ice cream to her people. Bags of candy and chocolate delights were also snatched up by the children.

Minutes after her arrival, Rose and other members of the immediate family were ushered into a private area. An unadorned pine casket was the central focus of the room. It was a fitting symbol for Helen; she was a simple woman. As each family member filed past saying goodbye, there was much weeping and wailing. It was clear that Helen, mother and friend to many, would be greatly missed. Rose held back her emotions; it was not her way to grieve. Her heart was aching, but in a silent way.

 Finally it was Rose's turn to see her Mom for the last time. Helen looked so beautiful; the innocence of girlhood was evident as she was dressed in her Navajo finery. Her hair was pulled back with a beautiful turquoise comb. She wore little makeup and her lips were dark. She wore a turquoise necklace, bracelet, and rings. Her blouse and skirt were purple, her favorite color. She also wore a woolen blanket coat and colorful shawl. She looked at peace and very beautiful – much like the black and white photo taken when she was a teenager.

With tears in her eyes Rose cried softly knowing this lovely Navajo Mother of many gave birth to her in 1950. Helen lived an honorable life, giving birth and caring for many children, grandchildren, and great-grandchildren. Helen only knew Navajo; she could not read or write. She gave birth to twin girls only to lose her twins because of a misunderstanding of language. Helen hoped and dreamed that one day she would be able to find her lost daughters. After thirty-three years, her wish came true in 1984. Rose cried because she knew Helen's first child, Mary Annette, chose not to meet Helen in this life but kept in touch through Rose. Their opportunity for reunion was not to be in this life. Still Rose brought something to honor the twins love for Helen. Rose carried two bouquets of identical flowers — one for Mary Annette, and one for Rose — to put on Helen's grave.

Many thoughts drifted through Rose's mind regarding the Navajo traditional way of death and burials. She was glad that the funeral was in the little LDS Mormon Chapel because she was of the same faith. She knew the Navajo People were not allowed to touch the dead, but she so wanted to give Mom a kiss or just touch her hand. Now all she could do was to look at this beautiful woman named Helen, her mother that gave her life and also taught her from afar who she really was.

Rose could not help visualizing Helen now looking down upon this group of people mourning her death. She believed that all who have passed on are looking on knowing that they are with those here in this life, too. In the Gospel of Jesus Christ, it is said that we are to be reunited with our loved ones, and we are only a thin veil away from this life.

Rose gave one more look before the last goodbye from the siblings. She marveled over how much they loved Helen. Levi helped Rose stand as she gave a prayer for the family prior to the closing of the casket. Then the official funeral started.

It was beautiful with many wonderful messages of love and respect for Helen. Rose learned many things about Helen that she had not known. Helen had been married three times, not twice. After Frank passed away; she met and married Mr. Chee. She bore two children, Wilson and a stillborn baby. Rose also learned some of Helen's nicknames to her children and grandchildren. "Basketball Girl" is Levyna, daughter of Levi and Emma Ben. She made the best fry bread around, was a good cook, and had a delightful sense of humor. Helen could dismantle a car engine and put it together in a short time. She challenged the young children to do this and had to come to their aid, as they couldn't put it back together and make it work.

Rose was happy to see AMAN Titus Haycock and Austin, both children of Louise. Both had many happy memories when first meeting the family. Austin was a little boy when Sister Johnson was serving on a mission in Phoenix. The family came to visit and swim at the pool. Even though she could not swim with them, they had a delightful time. Occasionally the family would have a picnic and play volleyball or baseball in a park. This brought the whole extended family for fun and relaxation with Rose.

Throughout the funeral, Rose was amazed at the sense of peace that permeated the room. When the service concluded, the family drove to the gravesite. Louise traveled with Lori and Rose to direct them.

With the winter snow and freezing cold weather, the Navajo Reservation roads stayed hard enough that their vehicle didn't slip and slide, but some vehicles did as they went up a small terrain to the gravesite. The site was not in a typical cemetery but a site where family members were buried. It is the same site where Helen's mother, Mabel Morgan, was buried only a few years earlier.

Funeral Services for Helen Ben
Pinon Branch, The Church of Jesus Christ
Of Latter-Day Saints, Pinon, Arizona
January 13, 2007 – 11:00 a.m.

Note: Prior to the funeral service family members were able to say their final goodbye; then Sister Rose
Johnson-Tsosie (daughter) gave the closing prayer prior to the sealing of the casket.

| | |
|---|---|
| Presiding: | Elder Michael Wintch |
| Conducting: | Elder Michael Wintch |
| Opening Hymn: | "There is a Green Hill Far Away." #3194 |
| Invocation: | Elder Jason Brignac |
| Eulogy: In Navajo | Elizabeth Morgan (Sister) |
| In English | AMAN, Titus Haycock (Grandson) |
| Comments: | Grandchildren (3) |
| Hymn: | Praise God from Whom All Blessing Flow" #242 |
| Remarks: | Elder Michael Wintch |
| Closing Hymn: | "God Be With You Until We Meet Again" #152 |
| Closing Prayer: | Elder Joshua Fellows |
| Pall Bearers: | Lawrence Ben (Son) |
| | Levy Ben (Son) |
| | Alison Ben (Son) |
| | Benjamin Ben (Son) |
| | Francis Ben (Son) |
| | Wilbert Tsosie (Grandson) |
| | Eduardo Hermosillo-Diuaz (Son-in-law) |
| Dedication of the Grave | Elder Michael Wintch |

Reception & Dinner to follow at the Ben Residence, Pinon, Arizona

Once at the gravesite, Rose, Louise and Lori got out onto the muddy ground. Fortunately, two sisters helped Rose find the way to the gravesite and kept her from slipping and sliding. The sisters seated her on one of three chairs and watched over her. Since she was the oldest child there she was considered more a "matriarch" and felt their love as they assisted her throughout the services. The gravesite was a traditional one with no adornment or headstones. As pallbearers helped take Helen's casket to the grave, snow started to fall. Rose's feet and hands were bitter cold; the coat she had on didn't keep the chills from coming. She was glad to sit down next to the gravesite.

Funeral Services for Helen Ben

## To Those I love and Those Who Loved Me
### Shared at the Funeral

When I am gone release me, let me go. I have so many things to see and so you must be not tie yourself to me with tears. Be happy that we had so many years.

I gave you my love. You can only guess how much you gave to me in happiness. I thank you for the love you each have shown, but now it is time I traveled on alone.

So grieve a while if you must, then let your grief be comforted by trust. It's only for a while that we must part, so bless the memories within your heart.

I won't be far away, for life goes on. So if you need me, call and I will come. Though you can't see or touch me, I'll be near.

On this solemn day a wonderful surprise came about when Rose heard her name whispered in conversation several times while walking to the gravesite.

"Are you sure it is Rose Johnson from Salt Lake City?"

Then, she heard, "I know a Rose Johnson, could it be the same?"

Only moments later did she find a wonderful lady standing in front of her saying, "Rose, I'm Judith Wintch."

That was all that Rose needed as she stood and hugged the unlikely stranger who knew her name.

What a joyful moment it was! Here was a lady that she knew in Salt Lake City, Utah, from the same professional group that she belonged to.

Both met monthly at a meeting for several years. Little did Rose know they would meet here as Judith's husband was conducting the funeral.

 Another miracle was that the Pinon Branch President was to officiate but was traveling. Therefore, Elder Wintch presided over the funeral. Was it by chance? No, to Rose nothing was by chance, it was meant to be.

Now Elder Wintch dedicated the grave with a prayer. Then, in keeping with Navajo tradition, all of Helen's possessions were buried with her body. Her clothes, shoes, and other items were put into the grave and covered with dirt. Each pallbearer took his turn in the service and with love and care, they covered Helen's body. In many Anglo funerals, the family walks away once the grave is dedicated. This is not the way with the Navajo. All members of the funeral party stay until the grave is fully covered and flowers are placed on the grave. Rose believed the patience and care of the Navajo way is a more respectful way.

After the grave was covered, Levi took a tree branch, wiped the graveside clean of clumps, and then placed a large floral arrangement on the gravesite. Rose placed the two bouquets on the grave. All walked away knowing Helen Ben was laid to rest and only those that were there would know where she was buried.

Rose explained to Lori while traveling back to Bahe's home about one of the Indian traditions known as "smudging." Once near Helen's home, the "smudging" ritual began. Each vehicle stopped, the people got out, walked through a burning fire of smoke, and washed with either Peyote water or herbal water. This ritual is intended to cleanse and bless those that attended the funeral.

They found their way into Helen's Hogan, where many family members had gathered. Traditionally, when one walks into a Hogan, he introduces himself by name to each individual as he walks in a clockwise direction around the inner circle. Once completed, both Lori and Rose sat on a bench. The gathering was for a Peyote Ceremony honoring Helen.

Very few Bilagaanas or white people are able to see a real Navajo Peyote Ceremony which can go on for several days. Rose did not believe in using Peyote and did not recognize the Navajo language, so she did not participate in this ceremony and left the Hogan. Once outside, they ran into several family members and stood in line for food. Two large tents were erected with a small wood stove for those eating to keep warm. One tent was for food service and one with covered tables for the guests. The food tent was so cold and the floors were very muddy. Rose was glad to hear one of her sisters invite them to go to the house where it would be warmer. The large wood stove was indeed welcomed for the warmth from the winter weather outside.

They ate and talked with Aunt Elizabeth and her sister Esther, who seemed so sad. One of the many traditions is no talking or seeing pictures of the dead. Rose had made a photo album for Bahe, Helen's husband, and showed the album to several family members in the room. When Esther saw some of the photos of Helen and Mabel, she said that she would tear them up and throw them away! Bahe held the book under his arm for sometime. Rose understood why. Some Navajos believe in this tradition, and some do not.

Stepping outside to clear her mind, Rose thought to herself, "Could tearing up a picture ever erase the memories that were seared into her heart and mind? Memories of a young mother and tiny twin girls…lost, then found. A few short years to try to make up for the many that were lost?"

The snow was beginning to fall. The ground around Helen's Hogan began to disappear under the cover a white blanket. It had been a long day – a difficult goodbye. Rose pondered the events that had brought her to this point. The journey home to be reunited with her mother after being separated at birth, the miracle of all the pieces falling into place to bring them together again, the many prayers that had been answered through the years. So many memories swirling around her like the snow circling over the Navajo landscape.

Then it came to her. She must tell this story. It must move from her heart to the page so that time would not cover it like the blanket of snow surrounding her. To honor her mother, a woman of such quiet strength, and the Heavenly Father who brought the miracle to pass, she would tell the story of Finding Helen – A Navajo Miracle.

To My Mother Helen,

"I love you… you are my mother that gave me life. I know you are in a better place now. I am confident that you are in the arms of our Heavenly parents: Father God and Mother Earth. -I visualize my adopted parents, Albert and Wilmont, welcoming you with open arms of love. My heart tells me that Frank, Mr. Chee, Mabel, and your babies that died early are with you now.

Helen, can you hear me? I hope so. It took 33 years to come home… it was a miracle. I remember that special day when we met. Oh how I loved seeing your beautiful face for the first time… I am humble and grateful to be a Tsosie. Though we could not speak the same language we did speak our hearts' desires. You taught me one of the great lessons in life… to believe in myself… to be thankful that I am a woman, a Navajo… most of all, to witness that God answered both our prayers. I wished not to be with you now, but to wait until one day when we will be together as a family again forever and ever. Until we meet again and I can touch your face again.

Helen Morgan Tsosie-Ben - Shima Nizohnnee, "beautiful mother."

Love, Your daughter

Rose Wyvette Johnson-Tsosie.

# FAMILY PHOTOS

Francis & Lorrette Ben

Evelyn & Helen 1984

The White House in Hyrum, Utah

Gordon Johnson & Family with Rose in 1993

Evelyn, Ben & family

Helen & Rose 2002

Helen with some of the children in 1984

Helen & the Girls in 1984

**Helen with Ben Children 1984**

**Helen with Grandchildren 1984**

**Helen with the Tsosie Children 1984**

**Family at LDS Dilkon Chapel**

Paul Tsosie & family 2002

Niece 2002

Lousie Tsosie

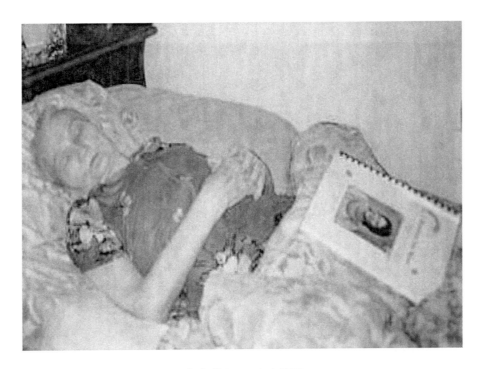

Judy Schwenchet 1999

Juanita & Evelyn 1984

107

Jim Mitchell & Family  with Sheila 1984

Paul Tsosie 1984

**Juaanita Wynette Tsosie**

**Francis & Lorrette Ben**

**Esther Tsosie**

**Emma (Levi) Ben**

Helen Morgan Tsosie-Ben
St. Patrick's Day – March 17, 1984
At Helen's Home, Pinon, Arizona

Helen Morgan Tsosie-Ben with daughter, Rose Wyvette Johnson-Tsosie
St. Patrick's Day – March 17, 1984
At Helen's Home in Pinon, Arizona

**Sister Rose Johnson-Tsosie with her Grandmother, Mabel Morgan**
**St. Patrick's Day, March 17, 1984**
**At Helen's Home, Pinon, Arizona**

Sister Rose Johnson-Tsosie with Paul Tsosie and Louise Tsosie
Visiting when Rose was serving in Holbrook/Phoenix Mission, Phoenix, Arizona
September 1984

Mabel Morgan and her daughter Helen Tsosie-Ben, 2000/2001

**Helen Morgan Tsosie-Ben, Navajo Rug Weaver**
It would take at least 9-12 months to do a rug this size. Many of her rugs were sold to various trading posts from Sedona, Arizona, Gallup, New Mexico.

**Rose Wyvette, Gordon, Desiree, Mary**
**At the Gordon & Lydia Johnson 50th Anniversary**
**June 2006**

**Rose with Lydia and Gordon**
**at their home in Bountiful,**
**Utah, 1994**

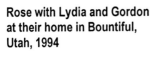

115

# Navajo Fashion Designer

Ms. Rose Tsosie Designs was hosted at the Embers gallery for a private show in early October to benefit The Spirit of Sharing, Inc. On October 18, 1982, there will be a public reception and showing of Ms. Tsosie's fashions at Embers, 1638 Ogden St., Denver.

Ms. Tsosie has recently moved to the Denver area from Washington, D.C. where she worked for 5½ years. "I want to design more western type clothing this year. Last year I had a lot of eastern wardrobe and now I've been here a year, I can see the casual but sophisticated look in wear. I'll not give up the formal evening wear and I think Denver will be pleased with the rich earth tones of my designs."

Tsosie style is simplicity and comfort. The colors are rich tones of red, purple and turquoise. Materials include raw silk, satin, taffeta and natural materials incorporated into not only victorian evening wear, but sleepwear, childrens wear, men's casual wear and costumes.

The designer uses Native American models and designs color and style to compliment the rich complexions of American Indians. She will also be showing modern traditional Native American dress design. The styles are not just for the boyish figure but all sizes of styles will be shown.

Tsosie designs began when Rose was only 5 years old in Arizona. She and her twin sister, now designing and residing in Florida, watched mother sewing everything for the family and home. An old treadle machine was given to the twins to occupy their time and allow them to learn. One would sew while the other worked the treadle.

Rose says that mother is still very active and influential in teaching young people sewing. She was the motivation the daughters needed to continue their designing and sewing through the years of school and careers by offering suggestions and new techniques.

For more information about Tsosie Designs and the public fashion show, call Embers at (303) 863-0131.

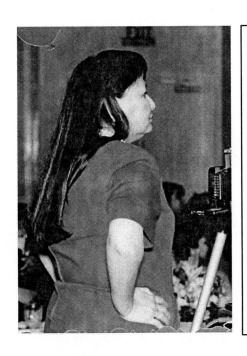

Rose

EPRI

Palo Alto,
California

1992 and 1993

Rose Johnson-Tsosie, Navajo Storyteller speaking at various organizations:

*Top Left- Right:* Toastmaster District 15 Fall Conference, SLC, Utah, 2006; Toastmaster International Convention, Phoenix, Arizona, 2007; Reid School, SLC, Utah, 2006; Tantalizing Tales at the Salt Lake Library, SLC, Utah, 2006.

Duane Evans, DTM - District 15 Governor presents Rose Johnson-Tsosie, DTM the Toastmaster Hall of Fame Award, Boise, Idaho 2001

Susan Baer, DTM – District 15 Governor presents Rose Johnson-Tsosie, DTM the Toastmaster Giant of the District Award, SLC, Utah, 2007

President Johnny Uy, DTM, Toastmaster International President, presents Rose Johnson-Tsosie, DTM, the Presidential Citation, Phoenix, Arizona, 2007

**Rose Wyvette Johnson-Tsosie**
Red Butte Gardens, Salt Lake City, Utah
2003

Photographer: Richard A. Etter, Ph.D. (Mentor and Friend)

# ADDENDUM

## A Visit with Judy
### November 21, 1999

One week before Thanksgiving, Rose had just completed attending a Toastmaster conference in Boise, Idaho. She didn't want to go anywhere just in case a phone call came in from Steve and Cindy Bixler. They would pick her up from the "Owyhee Plaza hotel then drive to Nampa where they lived. This special day, Rose would visit with Rhoda "Judy" Schwenkert, Cindy's grandmother, for the first time since 1951.

The Bixler family lived on a 33-acre farm in Nampa, Idaho. Twice Rose had talked on the phone with Cindy. Yes, forty eight-years had passed since both twins, Mary Margaret and Susan Rose, had stayed in the custody of Rhoda "Judy" who lived in Winslow, Arizona in the 1950's. Judy cared for the infant twins from the time they left the hospital until their adoption in August/September of 1951.

All Rose knew was her name, Judy Schwenckert. Judy also took care of another Navajo child, Dolly Goldtooth. Now she was about to learn more about Judy and learn more about her infant days.

Judy had called Rose about six months earlier on the phone.

"Is this Rose Johnson?" She asked.

"Yes."

"This is a voice from your past. Do you remember the name, Judy Schwenkert?"

"Yes," Rose nearly dropped the phone.

The two women talked just a few minutes. It was a miracle they had found one another via the Internet.

Through that telephone conversation, Rose learned of the nicknames, Madge and Midge, that Judy had given her and her twin.

Judy said that the Keams Canyon Hospital called her one day and asked if she could care for twin babies. She told them, "Only if they are Navajo." She was delighted to help care for twin babies. Madge and Midge were in her care for approximately 8 months.

Judy was born in 1909. She had married and had several children, then divorced and remarried later in life. Her husband passed away in March/April 1999. Both were actively involved in church and genealogy. She attended the LDS Boise temple as much as she could. Now Judy was ninety-years old. After the death of her second husband she lived by herself until just recently. Now she is staying with Cindy.

As Rose walked into Judy's room, she saw an elderly lady lying on a twin bed that was placed in the corner of the room. The first thoughts were of Mom in her later years, and Rose thought Judy looked more like Wilmont than she could have ever imagined. She was a small framed woman, fragile in weight. She was losing her hair, and the hair that was left was silver gray. She smiled even without her false teeth in place. Her hands and arms reached out toward Rose, bidding her to draw or come closer to her. As Rose bent over to give her a kiss on the cheek Judy made an effort to sit up, but she didn't have the strength.

"Oh my Little Midgee," Judy said. Rose could tell she wasn't as healthy as when they had talked on the phone six months ago. As she pulled a small wooden chair up near her bed, Judy explained her pain. She experienced Shingles and had open sores in her mouth and down her throat. She could hardly eat, and her physical strength was weakened. She wanted to put her false teeth in, but it would be too painful, so she hoped. Rose would understand. Rose watched her closely, knowing this would probably be the first and last time to see her in this life time.

Judy spoke of the days when Madge "the big one" would climb onto and into everything. Midgee would lay there, smile, and watch Madge stomp

123

around. She said she would liked to have kept us, maybe even adopt us, but with her limited income and knowing the twins would be better off with someone else, she just never did put in for adoption.

Dolly, another Navajo child was three or four months older than the twins. She was with Judy temporarily while her mother was in the hospital for Tuberculoses. Judy said that the state finally awarded Dolly to Judy though Dolly always knew her own family and where they lived. Dolly lived with Judy up until ten years ago when she returned to live on the Navajo Indian Reservation in Arizona. She hadn't heard from or seen her since.

Judy was delighted with the manuscript Rose gave her: "A Rainbow for Rose". She pulled the book close to her and read the caption. Rose was surprised that Judy didn't need glasses to read. Judy smiled as she looked at the photos in the book and said she would read the book immediately after Rose left.

Rose turned to a page with Annette's picture. Judy was pleased to see how beautiful Madge had become. It was humbling to see this little lady in her condition, and know how much she helped the twins after they left the hospital. Keeping the twins alive had been a challenge, but she did it. After Judy glanced over several photos, she sat the book down; it was getting too heavy for her. She looked straight at Rose and said, "I did the best I could for you girls. I'm glad I did – I helped you along the way."

Rose felt her sweet spirit and openly cried, expressing how much she loved her for taking care of them. They held hands, pondering their own thoughts. As Judy tried to turn on her side, Rose could tell she was in pain. She stated, "I don't know why the Lord wants me to be in pain; it's awful." For a flicker of a moment, oh how much she reminded Rose of Wilmont prior to her passing away.

The forty-five minutes was almost gone when Cindy appeared at the door way. Rose knew it was time to say goodbye. She didn't want to leave, but knew she had to.

Judy leaned forward and said, "Now I can sleep. I don't care to live anymore; I've accomplished it all."

Rose's emotions got the best of her, and she wiped her eyes. Leaning forward to give her a kiss, she whispered, "Goodbye. My prayers are with you always – I love you." She walked away, not looking back. Rose had the privilege to meet this sweet angel of a mother again and say goodbye.

She now had three wonderful mothers to love: Helen, Judy and Wilmont. Rose thanked God for the blessing of three great mothers who helped her along the way.

## *After Thoughts*

Rose looks forward to future trips to visit with family. She'll truly miss Helen and Mabel more than ever. Mabel passed away two years prior to Helen's death. Rose made a rush decision to come down after the burial. Evelyn Merrill drove her to visit the family. Our visit lasted only an hour, yet the effort was needed for Rose and her family.

*** 

Traveling takes a toll on Rose due to her diabetes. She also relates differently to her family because of her blindness. Using her white cane is hard because of the desert terrain. Still… it doesn't stop Rose.

*** 

Helen taught me one of life's greatest lessons — to be proud of my heritage and be thankful for life. I would not be here today if it hadn't been for Helen. After arriving home, Lynda Christensen said to me, "Rose, Helen is proud of you, she gave you life that you could accomplish what you have accomplished thus far," I cried.

Bahe Ben

Mabel and Helen

**The Herald Journal  Date: 05/05/99**
*Bridgerland's Daily Newspaper*

## *A Tale of Two Mothers*

Sign here said the doctor, and so she did, with an X and a thumbprint.

Come back for your babies in two months — was that the doctor's order? She wasn't sure for he spoke in English, not Navajo. But she knew her twin girls weren't well enough to leave the clinic with her. They weighed just three pounds, together.

January 1951 passed, then February. On March 1, the doctor looked up in surprise to see Helen. What did she want?

She had come for her girls, she said.

The doctor spoke, but Helen didn't understand. A translator joined them. Her girls were alive, he said, alive and gone. Given away, just like that.

Helen cried all the way home, in the wagon, in the rain. She was just 13, but already her heart had been broken.

Wilmont Johnson of Hyrum was all set to travel to Arizona to collect a baby when the phone rang. Instead of just one baby, would she and Albert be interested in twin girls?

Wilmont and her mother were soon on a bus in the desert, feeling very white amid the "Lamanite" passengers. Then they were in a room, advancing towards two cribs. The view from one crib has been preserved by its tiny occupant, Susan Rose.

"I remember exactly when my adopted mom and her mother came to take us up. I remember the smell and remember my mom coming toward me and her mother right behind her. I remember Mom coming over and pulling me up and grandma coming over and picking Annette up. I remember going out of the house, riding on the bus, seeing the land."

"You just went right to my heart," Wilmont told Rose.

On the way back with the twins, Wilmont and her mother felt whiter than ever, first on the bus in Arizona with Navajos, then on the bus in Utah with whites.

Wilmont had been a mother 14 years, to Gordon. But she had seen her two other infants die and knew she would not give birth again. Did that mean she couldn't have more children? Apostle Spencer W. Kimball, for one, thought not, and pointed her towards the Navajos. If there was a question, it was her age, 48.

Wilmont was getting older but would never be old. The woman was a whirlwind, much like Rose is today. Why, when she was picking up Rose and Annette, noticed another girl in the room. Would that girl care to come along, be adopted as well?

The quick answer was no, and so Wilmont had to be content with tinkering with the names of the twins. Mary Margaret became Mary Annette and Susan Rose became the rhyming Rose Wyvette.

True, there was a heart attack which temporarily stopped Wilmont's stair climbing. So she woke Rose and Annette with a whistle, one shriek for Annette, and two for Rose. Wilmont had her ways, one of which was to leave windows open, so brother it was cold up there.

The twins flushed toilets and rattled closet doors, all to keep Wilmont at bay and buy a little time under the covers.

But eventually they had to uncover and come down. Then it was 45 minutes on the piano for Rose, 45 minutes on the typewriter for Annette, after which they'd switch. Practice would be followed by readings from Wilmont, scripture and Shakespeare. Finally, it was off to school, South Cache and then Sky View, and in the evenings it was more piano and more typing, with tape hiding the letters on the keys.

"Very structured," Rose recalls. Now she herself is the same, very structured, as one must be if one is going to be an author, a fashion designer in New York, an FBI undercover agent and a regular at embassy parties and inaugural balls in Washington D.C., a speaker and earthquake survivor in California, a CPS in Salt Lake City, and a soon-to-be 30th reunion celebrant at Sky View.

She's been half her life away from Cache Valley, but just last week, dropping down from Wellsville and cruising across the green valley she said to herself "Home."

This was once her realm. After all, she and Annette were dairy princesses. There was no question as to who in the house was queen. "We not always agreed with Mom's thinking," wrote Rose. "Very outspoken," she said of her mother.

But without Wilmont's strength, where would they be?

"Mrs. Johnson," said the doctor, "you should have left these children on the reservation; they'll never be healthy and I doubt if the little one (Rose) will walk."

Would you expect Wilmont to wring her hands? You might as well expect her to stop sewing and take up smoking. What she did was take the girls for walks, down to the ducks, to the lambs, the calves. Down to see even the ants, who as workers had nothing on her and Albert.

As a shoe salesman, a farmer and a sugar factory worker, not to mention leather worker, a rug maker, a Utah State University gardener, and Rose's personal trainer, Albert was "always busy," Rose recalls.

He taught the girls to lasso and to love animals; Wilmont taught them to love books and love the Lord. With a year of college, she was an educator, sitting on her stool, reading aloud while the girls dressed and ate. How many other kids had the Bible with their breakfast? Wilmont had books and when they'd need more she'd take them to the library.

These library books went back, and the doughnuts - Wilmont's weakness - disappeared as well. But about everything else was saved, including the twins' hair which was saved from straightness by Wilmont's perms.

Wilmont saved enough dry and canned goods and bottled fruit for two years. But what she mostly saved was scraps of cloth, mountains of scraps. The Mode-O-Day lady she was called, after the dress factory.

With the scraps, he sewed up a storm, and so did Albert, even though he was going blind. Wilmont made bed sheets from flour sacks and underwear from sugar sacks. Inventive? She made pin cushions from tuna cans and step stools from tomato cans.

"She had a whole room just for sewing," Rose wrote. "Her room had a large mirror hanging over her favorite sewing machine, the Bernina. She had several other Bernina sewing machines in the room, along with a Pfaff machine too. Her closet was filled with supplies for sewing - bolts of material, volumes of patterns, needles, etc. Her desire was to teach everyone how to sew. She made beautiful embroidered towels, dresses and all types of clothes for all ages."

The girls were sewing by age five. Years later Rose was a star at a fashion show at New York's swanky Pierre Hotel. "Five women wore my designs. There were beautiful women wearing diamonds going up to them and asking where they could get those designs, Tsosie Designs. One lady wanted to fly me up to do her daughter's wedding.

"I thought of Mom and the beautiful things she used to make out of Mode-O-Day scraps."

Rose can't say that anything but hymns came from the piano. But the typewriters led to a Certified Professional Secretaries accreditation, and positions in Palo Alto, Calif. and Salt Lake City.

She almost never made it beyond Washington D.C. where she was almost killed, strangled, by the subject of the FBI investigation. It wasn't her first duel with death - as a little sliver of an infant; she almost never made it out of the Keams Canyon Hospital on the Hopi Reservation.

Her departure from that clinic was providential, and so may have been her return to the reservation.

Today when she thinks of Littleton, Colo. it is with grief because of what happened at the school down the road from where she lived. But back in 1983 living in Littleton was a gift, a launching pad for a church mission, her second.

At age 33, she was off to the Navajo Reservation.

One day a family Rose had been teaching approached her in church. "Do you know who you are?" they asked. "Yes," said Rose. "Do you know who you are?" they asked again. "If you found your mom would you be glad?"

So it came to be that Rose and several other missionaries were in the right place at the right time, at Helen Tsosie-Ben's dirt-floor Hogan when a blue truck drove up. One of the Navajo missionaries approached the woman on the passenger side and began to talk.

"The woman named Helen's eyes started to water and she smiled the most precious smile I've ever known. She rolled the window down and pulled me close to her as she could to give me a hug. Wow! A miracle was happening to me that day. I met my natural mother for the first time in 33 years, that's all I could think of. I heard a loud cheer from the missionaries."

Rose not only met her mother that day, she met her brothers and sisters, 14 of them. How would she ever remember their names? "The whole room was filled with family and missionaries all talking at the same time."

Her father had died after the birth of his twins, but Helen had remarried and had obviously gotten on with life. Yet on that very day, as every day, the lost twins were in her thoughts. She had been out once again trying to locate that paper with her X on it.

Driving along, something told her to return home. So she did and there was Rose.

Now that's faith. "Helen is one of the most believing people I've ever met," Rose says. "For 33 years she prayed for her lost babies." From Helen, she says, she learned "there is a plan."

When Rose says "prayed," she means prayed and prayed and prayed some more. One Thanksgiving Rose was asked to say a prayer, and she gave the customary two-minute rendition.

"I said 'Amen' and looked up but nobody moved. No one moved towards the food, no one did anything. I turned to one of my sisters and said 'Louise, how come nobody's eating?' She said, 'Our prayers usually last longer. Maybe two hours long.'

"I thought, What a wakeup call! They have nothing in the way of possessions, yet they can pray for two hours. It was a humbling experience.

They prayed for their grass, their land, their animals, their children. And I had prayed a tiny prayer. I thought it came from the heart."

In her heart, Rose finds no hardness towards the doctor who delivered her then took her away.

"He was wrong in giving the children away. Yet at the same time he gave us life. Annette and I would never have survived on the reservation. In his own way he was trying to protect us."

On Mother's Day, Rose as usual will visit Wilmont's grave. She'll send a gift to Helen, who won't leave the reservation. And she'll wonder about herself, as a mother.

"I know it will be," she says. "I know that's my blessing."

She was a mother once, to Annette's daughter Desiree back in 1975. A collision in Logan Canyon left Annette a widow; her husband Tyrone Douglas Young had been an admired administrator at Utah State University. Such were Annette's injuries that Rose had to leave the packed funeral service to attend her twin's surgery.

Little 9-month-old Desiree needed a mother and there was Rose. "I became very attached to her and I love her with all my heart. Maybe that was my time period for motherhood, taking care of Annette's child."

Annette has remarried and is a mother of three living in Portland, Ore. where she is employed by the Bureau of Indian Affairs. Rose is a conference coordinator at ARUP Laboratories in Salt Lake City, and is learning Navajo.

## About Rose

Many of Rose's life experiences are told as award-winning stories. Her goal is to publish the book, "Finding Helen - A Navajo Miracle." The book tells of her adoption and finding her natural family thirty-three years later. With her inspirational and humorous life experiences, it will be a book for all ages. In 1997, Rose was recognized in the book, "Surviving Two Worlds," in which she tells her story of adoption along with many other Native American people telling their stories while living in the non-Indian world. In 1972-73, she served her first full-time mission for the Church of Jesus Christ of Latter-day Saints in the California North Mission; a second full-time mission in 1983-1985 in the Arizona Holbrook (Phoenix) Mission; and third part-time service mission at the Family History Library in Salt Lake City, Utah. Rose is also a member of the Utah Storytellers Guild (Olympus Chapter).

Rose has been actively involved in Toastmasters International for over 18 years serving in leadership positions both in California and Utah. She received the Distinguished Toastmaster Award (DTM) in 2000 and 2006. She received the honored Toastmaster's Hall of Fame Award in 2002; Giant of the District in 2007, and the highest recognition, "The Presidential Citation," at the Phoenix convention in August 2007. She was a member of the California Speaker's Bureau (keynote speaker, seminar workshop leader, and inspirational speaker in youth detention centers, schools, churches, and civic groups). In 2001, she was a guest speaker at the Utah Museum of Natural History in Salt Lake City, Utah.

In 2002, Rose was diagnosed with Diabetes and Glaucoma. After six surgeries, with 97% peripheral vision loss, she is an advocate on health issues: Diabetic Complications: Blindness & Neuropathy.

In December 2003 her story, "Do Angels Live Here?" was published in the Desert Newspaper, Church News. Rose has also been actively involved in

the American Indian community in California and Utah.  In 2004, she was released as board member on the Indian Walk-In Center, Salt Lake City, Utah.  In 2005 and 2006, Rose completed a TV commercial for UCARE that is shown throughout the Wasatch Front.  She now resides in Bountiful, Utah. Rose is going on her third LDS mission as a "part-time service missionary" at the Family & Church History Center in September 2006.
*[Email: blindnavajo@hotmail.com]*

# GLOSSARY

**Burial (Navajo)** – Since Navajo families are matriarchal, the funeral arrangements are usually handled by the wife, mother or grandmother of the deceased. Some families care for their own dead with no funeral director involved.

The deceased is taken home and the following morning the body is placed on a board covered with a blanket, then taken to a church on Indian land for a service. The pallbearers are the only ones that can handle or touch the body and the grave. The home will need cleansing by smoke (the burning of a certain type of plant or bush). This ritual is usually performed by the medicine man. After the burial, all the family members gather for a meal; prior to that meal, portions of all the food items must be gathered to remember the spirit ancestors. The family may hold a three-day Peyote ceremony for family and friends.

In a Navajo burial service, funeral directors are requested since the Indian tradition is not to handle or touch the dead. First, a Navajo blanket is placed in the casket. The family provides two or more sets of clothing – one to be worn by the deceased, the second to be placed in the casket. Food, water and items that may have been valuable to the deceased also are placed in the casket.

The funeral service is conducted in both the Navajo and English languages. Family members may speak about the deceased to honor their beloved. All present must leave the church except for the immediate family, funeral directors and minister.

After the graveside service, the personal possessions of the deceased are put in the grave. Then the relatives (men) hold shovels filled with soil and all those in attendance walk around the grave counter clockwise sprinkling the dirt and placing flowers on the casket. If the casket is a sealer casket, the end cap is not placed on or the casket is not sealed so that the spirit may be released. After digging the grave, special care is taken to be sure that no footprints are left in or around the grave so the spirit guide will not take the wrong spirit.

**Clan Name** – When making introductions, a Navajo will tell his clan name, residence and occupation. There are four clan names in all - the mother's clan, the father's clan, the mother's father's clan and the father's father's clan.

**Cradleboard** – Navajo cradleboards are two connecting boards (approximately 24" X 14") forming the backboard with rawhide straps holding the child snugly to the board. The baby is wrapped in cloth and secured with rawhide ties. Many parents use the cradleboard to keep the baby safe till he is ready to crawl. Cradle-boards enable a mother to carry her baby on her back as she works or take the child along on horseback.

After the child's birth, the wood is chosen from the eastern side of a cedar or juniper tree that has not been struck by lightning, rubbed against by a bear, or broken by the wind. Cradleboards are thought to be a gift from the Holy People. The backboards represent mother earth and father sky. The head loop is bent like a rainbow to keep the child's head safe.

**Grandmother** – Mother's Side (Navajo amá sáni). Matriarchal family order in which the woman comes first before man.

**LDS Missionary** – Missionaries are representatives for the Church of Jesus Christ of Latter-day Saints in voluntary service. Pairs of young "Elders" serve two years and young "Sisters" serve 18-months. Older Sisters also serve alongside the younger sisters. Many Elders are recognized with black suits and white shirts carrying backpacks. Sisters usually wear dresses or a skirt and blouse. Some Elders walk or bike, while others drive. Sisters usually walk or drive a vehicle.

Sister Rose Johnson-Tsosie was called to serve as a full-time missionary from June 1983-January 1985 in the Arizona Holbrook/Phoenix Mission.

**Navajo Rug/Blanket** – Crafting a Navajo rug or blanket takes time, skill and talent. It starts with raising the sheep for the wool, then many months of preparation and weaving to have a finished product to keep or sell. Sheep shearing is an art as the sheep is stripped of its wool from head to tail. The wool is then cleaned and washed with yucca, then dried in the sun. Once dry, the wool is carded. If gray wool is desired, then white and black are carded together. Next, the spindle is used to make the yarn and thread to the desired thickness. Sometimes it takes spinning the wool over and over again, up to a dozen times to make it strong. Various plants such as: cactus, chokecherries, grape, thistle, and various berries are used to dye the wool. These are ground up and the wool is dipped into the buckets of color many times to achieve the correct shade. The next step is setting up the loom(s). For a small weaving it could take up to a couple of months. For Helen's blanket/rugs it could take up to 9 months. The weaving takes place throughout the day amid many other chores and responsibilities. Once completed, the rugs are sold to the trading post(s) for a small amount of money considering all the work that was involved.

**Navajo Rug Types (Helen and sisters have made rugs, example):**

- **Two Gray Hills Rug**: Earth tones and natural wool colors of gray, white, black and brown predominate in "Two Gray Hills" rugs; they usually have a central diamond pattern with four equal triangle shapes at the corners.

- **Storm Pattern:** Showing four stepped lines representing lightning radiating from a central rectangle is characteristic of western reservation rugs from areas such as Tuba City. A block in each corner of the rug represents the four sacred mountains.

**Piñon** – (Navajo: *Be'ek'id Baa Ahoodzání*) is a census-designated place (CDP) in Navajo County, Arizona, U.S.A., and in the Navajo Nation. The population was 1,190 at the 2000 census. Helen lives approximately four miles south of the Pinon water tower just prior to arriving in Pinon. These areas consist mostly of rugged, dirt roads.

**Puberty Ceremony (Kinaalda)** – When a Navajo girl reaches the age of twelve and experiences her first menstrual cycle, she becomes initiated into womanhood by a beautiful four day ritual entitled the *Kinaalda*, also called the *Navajo Blessing Way* Ceremony. The term *Kinaalda* literally translates as "puberty ceremony," and is interchangeable with both the male and the female ceremony.

Based on a myth about the first *Kinaalda,* performed by and for the Changing Woman, who is the female deity identified with the Earth. She is the source and sustenance of all life on the earth, controlling particularly fertility. The ceremony is a bridge, a rite of passage, to womanhood.

**Roadman** – The Native American Church (NAC) considers the "roadman" a spiritual minister who helps with the "Peyote" ceremony. A traditional tipi is put up and taken down by the roadman's help. He is a servant with various responsibilities in the spiritual ceremony.

**Shepherd's Plate** – is the first plate of prepared food and drink for those tending the sheep. A "shepherd's plate" is also prepared for a visitor to take home with them, especially if they were traveling a long distance. If a guest left the home without the plate it could be considered an act of disrespect on their part.

**Smudging** – A way of using the smoke from burning either a Cedar, Sage, Sweetgrass or Pinon Pine, to cleanse (purify) a person of negative influences. It is considered desirable to have "good" way or energy. When the plant is cut, prayers for healing or energy should be offered and thanks given to the plant for its use.

**Truck** or vehicle/large truck – (Navajo: *chidi'tsoh*). Many Navajos are known for the vehicles they drive, especially the truck. Often families go into debt just for their "big" vehicle(s).

**Wash** *or gully* – (Navajo: cháshk'eh) When rain water develops on the reservation road so that it become impassable. The dirt roads throughout the Navajo reservation are unusable when the rain or snow makes the roads slippery and water builds into a gully. When you come upon a wash you must speed up to get across or make a new trail around the wash. In any case, the road(s) you depend upon can change immediately if the weather is unfavorable.

**Yeibechai** – In the fall, a costumed figure called the Yeibechai comes out. He may be dressed in a headdress and carry a rattle. Traditionally he is entitled to take something that belongs to you if there is no offering given to him. In recent years, the Yeibechai have begun to collect for worthy causes.

The "Bluewater" Clan
Killen, Alabama – March 2008
"We worked hard and had Fun!

Macolm & Angela Broyles + Extended Family;
Sandi Harvey; Duane Evans and Mr. Eddie
Thank You!

Bluewater Publications is a multi-faceted publishing company capable of meeting all of your reading and publishing needs. Our two-fold aim is to:

1) Provide the market with educationally enlightening and inspiring research and reading materials.
2) Make the opportunity of being published available to any author and or researcher who so desires to become published.

We are passionate about preserving history; whether it is through the re-publishing of an out-of-print classic, or by publishing the research of historians and genealogists; Bluewater Publications is the peoples' choice publisher.

For company information or for information about how you can be published through Bluewater Publications, please visit:

**www.BluewaterPublications.com**

Also, to purchase any of the books we publish, you can find them on Amazon.com.

*Confidently Preserving Our Past,*
Bluewater Publications.com
Formerly Known as Heart of Dixie Publishing